FISHING IMPOSSIBLE

FISHING IMPOSSIBLE

THREE FISHING FANATICS. TEN EPIC ADVENTURES.

WITH BLOWFISH, CHARLIE AND JAY

AND DAVID BARTLEY

ATLANTIC BOOKS

Published in hardback in Great Britain in 2016 by Atlantic Books,
an imprint of Atlantic Books Ltd.

10 9 8 7 6 5 4 3 2 1

A CIP catalogue record for this book is available from the British Library.

Hardback ISBN: 9781786491169

Printed in Poland on behalf of Latitude Press

Atlantic Books
An Imprint of Atlantic Books Ltd
Ormond House
26–27 Boswell Street
London
WC1N 3JZ

www.atlantic-books.co.uk

CONTENTS

FOREWORD

I n the *Compleat Angler*, first published in 1653 and the second most reprinted book in the English language after the *King James Bible*, Izaak Walton sums up fishing's timeless appeal: *'God never did make a more calm, quiet, innocent recreation.'* No doubt. But this isn't that kind of fishing.

Take an airline pilot, an ex-Royal Marine Commando-turned-social worker and possibly the world's only heavy-metal marine biologist, and what have you got? Three fish fanatics who take it in turns to challenge each other to catch their chosen quarry, in some of the most unorthodox ways possible. Tough assignments though these prove to be, each is the culmination of a long-cherished dream. An impossible one? Are they trying to catch the uncatchable? We'll see.

In the ten adventures in this book, based on the television series of the same name, Charlie Butcher, Jay Lewis and the man they know only as 'Blowfish' travel to some of the world's most spectacular, inaccessible and dangerous places. Charlie with rod and line, Jay with a spear-gun, Blowfish with his bare hands. At times in competition and at times together, their mission is to catch some of the most challenging fish on the planet.

The three travel to the Great Bear Rainforest in British Columbia, after the silvery coho salmon; to the Bahamas, to wage war against the invasive red lionfish; and to Lake Turkana, in the middle of a Kenyan desert, to seek the mighty Nile perch. In Thailand, they meet the 'Sea Gypsies' and spear-fish for the fearsome giant Moray eel; travelling to the southern tip of Argentina they hope to become the first ever amateurs to catch the elusive Patagonian toothfish; and off the coast of Peru they hunt the mighty Humboldt squid. Much further north, they head to Scapa Flow, in Orkney, to catch fish in freezing cold water among the ghostly wrecks; and further still to Norway, to visit the court of king crab. In warmer waters, they travel to Laos, after the rare devil catfish, and to the tip of South Africa, hoping to get to grips with the great white shark. Welcome to *Fishing Impossible*.

The catch here is not just that the fish do not particularly wish to be caught: there are other interested parties involved. Bears, crocodiles, scorpions, seals, sharks, and the worst the elements can throw at a defenceless human being, in some of the most inhospitable spots on earth. The intrepid trio might not be in danger of being sawn in half by a powerful laser or shot at by extras armed with machine guns, but this is James Bond with a rod, line and spear.

Fishing is a living for many and a vital source of food for all. But not everyone sees the point of it as a pastime. Dr Johnson is supposed to have defined a fishing rod as 'a stick with a hook at one end and a fool at the other'. Many fishermen have felt that way after a day spent fruitlessly casting again and again. Never mind the enjoyment of the process or the attractiveness of the scenery: getting the fish into your hands is the main event. Hook now, to avoid disappointment.

To succeed at fishing you need to understand the natural history – the feeding and breeding habits of each species of fish; whether they take bait, and if so what sort; where they like to hunt; the habits of their prey, and predators; the local terrain, the local weather; and the relative health of the waters. Charlie, Jay and Blowfish work closely with local guides, and so in every case they learn something about the culture and the history of the extraordinary and beautiful places they're lucky enough to be fishing in.

This series is *Fishing Impossible*, not *Fishing Irresponsible*. It's about celebrating the extraordinary species that inhabit the waters of our planet – not harming them. So wherever in the world the team were, ethical and responsible fishing was at the top of the priority list.

Along with the obvious things like following local regulations and catch limits, and handling the fish safely and correctly, *Fishing Impossible* was guided by the principle that if you catch a fish, you put it back, unless it's going to good use.

Much of the fishing in *Fishing Impossible* was inherently dangerous. But not reckless. Not always seen on camera were the battalions of safety personnel of all kinds – in and out of the water – who made sure Jay, Charlie and Blowfish came back from these adventures in one piece. Discretion is the better part of valour!

'Give a man a fish and you feed him for a day: teach a man to fish and you feed him for a lifetime,' the old proverb has it. Or, as the American humorist Zenna Schaffer put it: 'Teach a man to fish and you can get rid of him for the whole weekend.' Fishing is a most absorbing sport.

BRITISH COLUMBIA

THE LOCATION: BRITISH COLUMBIA, CANADA

THE FISH: COHO SALMON

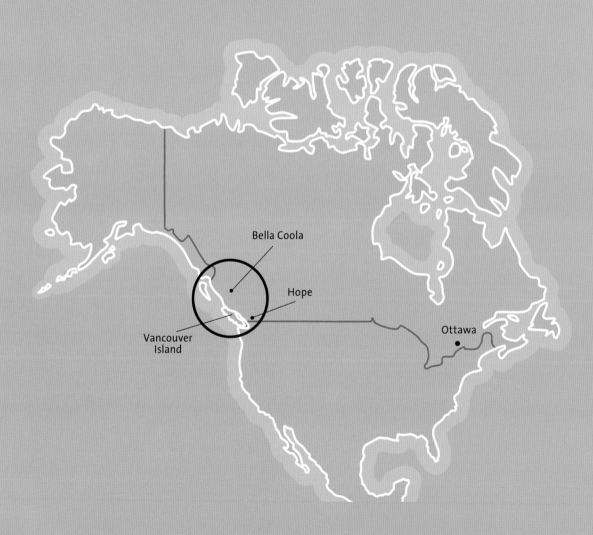

CHARLIE IS A FLY-FISHING NUT, a dedicated rod and line man, so it's no great surprise that his challenge to Blowfish and Jay is to catch some salmon. But not just any salmon. They're after the coho, a legendary addition to any fly-fisher's bucket – and bucket list. To find their quarry the boys are travelling to one of the most spectacular, austerely impressive rainforests in the world – but not a tropical one. Charlie, Blowfish and Jay are headed for British Columbia in western Canada, to the world's biggest temperate rainforest. To fish for the salmon here the boys will need to brave the rigours of the North American wilderness, like *The Revenant's* Hugh Glass, Kit Carson and the fur trappers and frontiersmen of two centuries ago.

Charlie cut his teeth fly-fishing in the beauty of the Scottish Highlands. British Columbia, with almost a million square miles of snow-capped mountains, pine, spruce and cedar forests, green valleys, and lakes and rivers bursting with salmon, is 'Scotland on steroids'.

Catching coho here requires some performance enhancement too, and not only because the coho are the toughest and strongest of all the Pacific salmon. Fishing here means the boys are in competition with the finest, but least friendly, salmon fishers anywhere on the planet: Charlie, Jay and Blowfish are heading into the heart of the Great Bear Rainforest.

Because of recent droughts and a lack of snowfall, the only viable place to fish for coho is up in the mountains – the home of the formidable grizzly bear.

And so the first challenge Charlie has set the *Fishing Impossible* team is this: they each need to come up with a foolproof method to catch fish from under the bears' noses, while keeping out of harm's way. And that won't be child's play.

CHARLIE:

'FISHING IMPOSSIBLE ISN'T JUST ABOUT FISHING – IT'S ABOUT BEING IN THESE BEAUTIFUL, SPECTACULAR PLACES, WHERE THE FISH ARE WILD AND CHALLENGING. FOR ME, TO HUNT A BEAUTIFUL FISH THAT'S GROWN UP LIVING IN A HARSH ENVIRONMENT IS WORTH CATCHING 50 MILLION FISH THAT ARE STOCKED. GOING INTO THESE WILD PLACES AND CATCHING A CREATURE THAT'S NOT TAME; THAT'S WHEN YOU FEEL A REAL SENSE OF ACCOMPLISHMENT. AND THEN YOU PUT IT BACK.'

In their quest for the coho, Jay, Blowfish and Charlie will be tracking the salmon's journey from the open sea to the upper reaches of the river in which the fish were born. Team *FI* ease into the programme with a little light fishing where no bears are likely to trouble them, unless they are exceptionally good swimmers – out in the ocean, off the western coast of Vancouver Island. Here the Pacific salmon, in their millions, pass through on their way to fresh water. Here, too, their predators await – halibut, ling cod and rockfish – and it's these hunters that Blowfish, Charlie and Jay are after. Hiring kayaks, the craft used for millennia by the 'First Nations', the indigenous peoples here, they start their journey in a traditional manner, by way of a training exercise. Some form of rod and line fishing – Charlie assumes – will be essential for catching the coho way upriver. And Blowfish has never fished before.

Introducing anyone to fly-fishing for the first time is a joy for a seasoned fisherman. Traditionally, however, it is children, and not heavy-metal-loving marine biologists. Blowfish has serious trouble adapting to the idea of sitting still, waiting, and watching. Charlie's quiet ideal of dangling the line and hoping for a bite doesn't quite fit the action-packed lifestyle of free-diving Jay, but the passivity pays off – Jay hooks a beautiful yellow eye rockfish, quickly followed by Blowfish catching a translucent vermilion rock cod. The luck of beginners …

In recent years the yellow eye rockfish and some other species have decreased in numbers quite rapidly in these waters. These fish don't reach sexual maturity until between ten and twenty years of age. (They can live until they're over 100 – some Methuselah-like specimens staggering on to 147.) If too many young fish are killed, the very existence of a next generation is under threat. So there is a voluntary quota in place, with only a small number to be caught by each angler who subscribes to it. Another reason to limit the catch is that, if hooked and brought to the surface, fish like the yellow eye cannot be released back into the water. Doing so would be a death sentence.

SWIM BLADDERS

THE BLOWFISH FILE

Yellow eye rock fish, vermilion rock cod and many other species of fish have a 'swim bladder', a gas-filled sac which allows the fish to regulate its buoyancy, so it can remain at its chosen depth without needing to expend energy swimming.

But just to say that the swim bladder is a buoyancy aid hardly does justice to the remarkable variety of uses that different species have found for it. Some wobble their swim bladders, and others drum on them, in order to communicate. In the remarkable case of herrings, the swim bladder is linked to their ears, greatly improving their hearing range and sensitivity. Herrings also produce what scientists have dubbed (with either conscious or unconscious humour) fast repetitive tics, or 'FRTs', that the swim bladder emits through their anal vents – to send messages to their colleagues, through both sound and chemical signals.

As the fish is reeled in from depth, the swim bladder simply cannot deflate fast enough to compensate. As it rises to the surface, the decrease in depth, and therefore decrease in pressure, causes the swim bladder to rapidly expand, pushing the internal organs out of the mouth and anus, mortally wounding the fish.

This rapid ride to the surface usually kills the fish, but if you do see any signs of life, euthanasia is the only option – you have to be prepared to kill the animal swiftly and respectfully. You don't mess around when fishing for rock cod. If you're going to try for them at all, fish smart, and fish only for what you are prepared to eat.

One fish supper later, Jay, Charlie and Blowfish move inland. They travel up the mighty Fraser River – British Columbia's longest – from its estuary near Vancouver to a place called, and this is surely a good omen, *Hope*. It's time for Charlie's superior experience in the arts of coarse fishing to really come to the fore now. Because he and Jay are after the biggest fresh-water fish in the whole of North America, the white sturgeon.

White sturgeon have been around for a million years, if not more. They can live to be 100 years old, getting fat on the millions of salmon making their way upriver. And the white sturgeon is a leviathan. The biggest ever caught, in 2012, weighed in at 498.9 kilograms and measured 3.76 metres, and it was bagged by an Englishman, in the Fraser River. Like every keen fisherman, Charlie would be delighted if he could best this record.

However, hope looks like it might be in short supply: Charlie and Jay could hardly have chosen worse weather to fish in if they'd done it for a bet – torrents of rain are lacerating the river. Fishermen are used to the cold and the wet, to standing in grim conditions patiently waiting for their catch, but when you've travelled this far the weather is a little disheartening. But Charlie's luck suddenly changes – he is on. Thrilled it's not a false alarm – whatever's on the end of the line, there's a hundred or so kilos of it, and it's racing away like the clappers. This can only be an encounter with the legendary white sturgeon.

CHARLIE'S NOTEBOOK

The foremost principle behind any type of fishing is blindingly obvious: fish where the fish actually are. To locate them is a combination of fishing at the optimum time of day and in the optimum place. Put like that, it sounds easy: it isn't. 'Watercraft' is always at a premium – looking for the subtle signs that might give away the presence of the fish you're after. But in virtually every case, if you're fishing in unfamiliar territory, the inside track is to seek local knowledge and ask the experts. Such as Kevin Estrada, our skipper on the Fraser River, with ten years' experience of fishing for sturgeon under his belt.

Kevin pointed us towards the places where the sturgeon would most likely be fishing themselves. (We were using salmon eggs for bait.) The best bet was that they would be found in shallower, slightly calmer pools, away from the main driving current. It paid off: our fish were caught in the bend of a river.

Because white sturgeon are so powerful, it's vital to let the line play out until the fish has tired, or it will snap the line. You then start reeling in until the fish gets a second wind and hares off again. And repeat the process, until it's too exhausted to fight on.

With a fish this size, you need a boat (with someone to steer it); a strong, cushioned rod to absorb the impact; and a reel with a 'drag', or gearing mechanism, which controls the tension on the line. If the line is too tight it will snap; too loose and the fish won't tire.

Overall, you're looking for a well-balanced, nifty combination of kit, to give you maximum flexibility of movement; what anglers like to call 'a nicely weighted outfit'.

These fish are heavyweights – reeling them in is like going twelve rounds with Mike Tyson. Several times during the bout, Charlie has looked down at his reel and found it's completely out of line, so strongly is the fish racing away. The boat has to chase after it, or the line will snap. In the end it takes Charlie forty-five minutes to bring the sturgeon in. By the time it's been landed, it's pulled the boat two miles down the river. But the chase has been worth defying the elements for: at 2.1 metres and around 78 kilograms, this is the biggest fish Charlie's ever caught. And, by a factor of a hundred, the one that's fought the hardest. It will do so another day, perhaps: after being unhooked and measured, it goes straight back in the water.

Jay, having watched Charlie's efforts patiently, finally gets his turn to hook a sturgeon. And it fights its corner just as hard as Charlie's did. When it's reeled in – after an hour – it's bigger still, at 2.43 metres long and a shade under 136 kilos. That's the weight of a fat man, or a small bear. Jay's catch is a 'virgin sturgeon', one which has never been caught before. To help collect conservation data – if it's caught again – it's duly fitted with an electronic tag before being released.

The next day the team set off for their final fishing adventure of this trip. They cram into a tiny plane – imagine a flying Robin Reliant – to make a buccaneering, white-knuckle, sick-inducing journey over the mountains to the Bella Coola Valley, right in the heart of the Great Bear Rainforest. It's stunning. To Charlie it feels like the end of the world – beautiful, wild, flooded. To have all this served up with the chance to catch the elusive coho salmon is a dream come true.

But the reason the team have risked life and limb to fly here, and why they are risking life and limb to fish cheek by jowl with the bears, isn't just because of the spectacular scenery. They're also here because a reduction in the amount of snowfall last winter, followed by warmer spring temperatures – attributed by most scientific observers to climate change – has led to lower water levels and higher water temperatures than are normal. This has caused some salmon to die far earlier in the course of their journey upriver than they should do, either because of weakened immune systems and a higher risk of infection, or because they were forced to make a last-ditch detour to cooler waters. The Bella Coola Valley has been chosen because the 'snow-pack' here has, thankfully, provided sufficient melt-off to make the salmon run viable.

THE SALMON RUN

The Pacific salmon run is the largest transfer of nutrients from ocean to land anywhere in the world. You've got the fish feeding on crustaceans, molluscs and other fish. Then you're taking all those nutrients, all those minerals, and smashing them deep into the forests. It's the best fertilizer you could get. As much as 80% of the nitrogen needed for these trees to grow comes from the salmon. These are salmon forests.

The life cycle of the Pacific salmon is truly extraordinary. After the eggs have hatched in the gravel streams upriver, the young coho spend about a third of their lives in fresh water before heading out to sea. Here they mature, and then spend the final third of their lifespan back in the rivers in which they were born. Typically the coho live for three years, sometimes two or four.

In order to move from fresh water to salt water and back again, a whole series of startling physiological changes takes place. As they reach the sea, salmon start to drink copious amounts of salt water in order to keep hydrated. What's hard to credit is that the fish can actually desalinate the salt water. The kidneys dramatically reduce their production of urine so as to conserve as much H_2O as possible, while excess salts are forcibly excreted by special chloride cells in the gills. The salmon are making fresh water in their own bodies.

On returning to the natal stream, the salmon stop drinking completely, and their kidneys produce large amounts of urine so as to rid their bodies of excess water, which is now rapidly being absorbed into them. Salt is now precious and is being stripped from the salmon by the incoming fresh water, so the chloride cells in the gills now pump salt *in* so as to compensate, while the kidneys reabsorb what they can from the urine.

The evolutionary idea behind this incredible journey is that salmon that spawn in fresh water are putting their eggs far, far away from the many predators of the ocean.

So just the basics of staying alive are using up vast amounts of energy. But it doesn't stop there. As salmon mature (into grilse), a physical transformation takes place. Silver while out at sea, the male salmon now develop canine teeth and a hooked mouth (called a 'kype') to equip them for the battles with other males that lie ahead. And, in the case of some species, they grow humps. They change colour, the coho males turning a bright red, and developing green markings on their backs and heads. The females change colour too, but less dramatically.

This heavy-duty wardrobe change takes its toll: it uses up precious energy. But there's a good reason for this expenditure. Reproduction. These changes in appearance on the part of the males are for one thing only: to impress the females, showing that they have sufficient energy to laugh off the herculean efforts involved in these physiological transformations.

All this effort, transformation and travel would wear down the strongest man, and you might think that some serious eating is needed to sustain it. But no. This miracle of nature is all conducted on the ultimate crash diet: once they enter fresh water the salmon don't eat anything at all. In fact, their stomachs disintegrate. This is to make way for more muscle, and, for males and females respectively, for sperm and eggs.

Another crucial sign of a male salmon's fitness as a mate is its ability to 'site select'. In any salmon river there is a limited amount of available nutrients and space, and optimum water flow. So the strong male salmon identifies the best breeding area, and protects it against all comers. The females know a prime breeding site too when they see one, and will happily mate with whichever male is currently sitting pretty on the best spot. But with their energies sapping, they need to get straight down to business.

The female digs a small depression in the gravel, called a 'redd', by fanning her caudal, or tail, fin. She then lays the first batch of eggs, which the male quickly fertilizes. The female then moves upstream to dig another redd and the process is repeated until she is out of eggs (there may be six or seven redds in all). The gravel excavated for each subsequent redd flows back downstream to cover the previous one, burying the eggs and protecting them from hungry mouths. Having laid all her eggs, the female dies. The male, if he is still up to the task, may now mate with other females. But eventually, he'll run out of steam too. After their deaths, the adult salmon's bodies will bring life to a whole ecosystem, while the next generation grows in the gravel.

FACT FILE

NAVIGATION – SHOW ME THE WAY TO GO HOME

Salmon live and hunt thousands of miles out in the open ocean. So when they decide to return to the rivers they were born in it's not a simple journey. Just what is it that guides them back to their home?

Tidal factors may come into play, along with the salmon reaching their optimum size, but it's now believed that they can navigate back to their natal rivers by 'magnetoception', a kind of built-in GPS using the Earth's magnetic field. Tiny little lumps of iron have been found in the brains of some salmon species. Once they get close to the river, they use their extremely acute sense of smell to sniff out and home in on the exact area of the river in which they themselves began life. At least, that's the idea. But it doesn't always work in practice, and some of the salmon will find themselves ending up in rivers they weren't born in. This is no problem, though, as there are still plenty of salmon to spawn with, and it has the added bonus of swapping around some genes with different populations, thus keeping the whole species healthy.

So now the coho challenge begins in earnest, particularly as the Bella Coola Valley is Grizzly Bear Central, the densest concentration of them in all of British Columbia, with one grizzly to every fifteen people. Their ubiquity is brought home with a bump within thirty minutes of landing: the team see a mother grizzly right by the side of the road. And then another. The jokes are over; this mission has to be taken seriously.

To find out what they're up against, Jay, Charlie and Blowfish get some advice from Holly Willgress, a former environmental biologist who now runs adventure tours and bear-watching trips in the rainforest. Following tracks through the woods, they find a huge grizzly paw-print, clearly showing the indent of its lethal claws.

Holly reassuringly declares that attacks from bears are rare. When they do happen it's mostly when the bear is startled, or defending its food or its cubs. But hungry bears can be predatory, and unpredictable. Like humans, bears have moods. A young 'subordinate' male bear, for example, if he's been kicked around by a more dominant male, may well be in an extremely bad mood, which makes him more likely to attack than to run away.

Holly has had her own nerve-racking encounters with grizzlies, but only when she was younger, less experienced and doing something idiotic and dangerous. Fishing for salmon in bear-infested waters was unfortunately one of those times. The boys will need to be careful.

Holly's advice on what to do when a bear comes for you is to back away slowly. And if it keeps coming, to stand your ground, as running away might only inspire the grizzly's hunting instincts further, and it may start a chase. This is where a tube of bear-spray comes into play; an industrial-strength 'pepper spray' (which does no lasting harm), it is made from capsaicin, the chemical that makes

FACT FILE
SO JUST HOW DANGEROUS ARE BEARS?

Anyone who's seen *The Revenant* will know that if a grizzly bear takes a fancy to you it's not the animal that's likely to come off worse. Their claws are razor sharp, and one swipe of their paws can kill. They're powerful enough to bite into you and shake you around like a rag doll, to say nothing of smashing into your SUV and making off with your picnic sandwiches. Grizzlies can run as fast as 40mph over short distances, and grow to up to 450 kilos at the top limit. Most females weigh around 135 kilos, and the males, 180 kilos.

Grizzlies – *Ursus arctos horribilis* – are a sub-species of the brown bear. They arrived from Asia by crossing the land bridge that used to connect with Alaska in what's now the Bering Strait. There are nearly 14,000 grizzlies in British Columbia, around half the number there were two centuries ago. Although some are deliberately killed each year by humans (hunting grizzly bears is still allowed here, strange to say, albeit under a strict licensing and quota system), and others are killed in road or rail accidents, the biggest threat comes from our encroachment into their habitat. A fully-grown male grizzly needs a home range of up to 700 square metres in which to find food, mates, and sites in which to dig dens.

One of the greatest hazards for bears in recent years is that they have become increasingly attracted to the smell of cooking, and leftovers thrown into the dustbin, particularly hungry bears that are struggling to find natural sources of food. This is of course a threat to humans, who might find a bear right on their doorstep happily raking through their rubbish; but it's even more of a threat to the bears. While a grizzly that kills a human is usually destroyed, it's never the other way round. So if we don't take sufficient care with our cooking and waste disposal methods, the tab for our folly and carelessness will be picked up by the animals themselves. Despite their reputation for fearsome attacks on humans, in their dealings with us they nearly always come out on the short end.

chillies 'hot'. Effective within 9 metres, the trick is to aim above the bear's head so the spray falls into its naval cavities and puts it off its stroke. Then run.

Autumn is the bears' peak feeding season, as hibernation approaches, so the appearance of salmon is most welcome. They don't eat the whole fish, but favour the fattiest items – the skin, brain and ovaries – which will give them the fat reserves, and thus stores of energy, to last them through the winter. What the bears don't eat once they've filleted the salmon isn't wasted: it goes on to play a vital role in the ecology of the rainforest itself.

The boys have all dutifully met Charlie's initial challenge and come up with their own cunning methods to catch salmon without having to exit, pursued by a bear. Charlie himself has chosen an elaborate hide – which looks like a bubble car that's been smothered in glue and driven backwards through a charity shop. Jay's idea is to fish from up in a tree, out of the way of the bears, using a traditional lumberjack's spurs and harness. (No one has the heart to tell him that grizzly bears can, actually, climb trees.) Blowfish has chosen to fish in a fancy-dress outfit. Not disguised as Superman or Mother Teresa, but as a 'Kermode' bear – a sub-species of the black bear. The Kermode, or 'spirit bear', is white, or cream-coloured. A tenth of black bears are born this way. They're found only in the Great Bear Rainforest.

Blowfish's idea has solid science behind it, of course: white bears cast less of a shadow than black bears, and this reduces the likelihood of frightening off the fish. It's been suggested that because of this, spirit bears catch around a third more salmon than do their darker cousins.

So there's plenty of method swirling around amid all this madness. And yet, strange to relate, none of these ingenious wheezes work – not in the slightest. There's only one thing for it now: the boys are going to have to get into the water – bears or no bears.

After what seems like hours – and *is* hours – the fish just aren't biting. There's no doubt that Charlie and Jay – Blowfish having retired to the bank, happy to watch the lack of drama from dry land – are in the right place. They know this not just because all the subtle, tell-tale signals are present and correct – the 'watercraft'. Another important clue is that the coho are actually leaping out of the water, waving their fins at them in derision. Charlie's run of bad luck in British Columbia can't be shaken off, so the inevitable happens. The luck of the Cornish strikes. Jay's coho is a beauty. The mission has been accomplished: the team have caught their coho. And none of them have been eaten by bears – as yet. So, with the points in the bag, it surely doesn't matter who scored? Charlie, as team captain, puts a brave face on it. But inside, he is wrestling with the dread serpent of despair.

All anglers brood after a day when their luck just wasn't in. What did I do wrong, where did my tactics fail? What did I do to offend the gods? What terrible crime did I commit in a former life? How can I ever show my face in human society again? Meanwhile the bait, the tackle, the weather, the quality of water … all of them, loudly protesting their innocence, are dragged into the dock.

But success is all the sweeter because of the failures in between. The real art of fishing is to learn from your experiences, bad and good. And there's precious little pleasure or satisfaction in rocking up somewhere just to shoot fish in a barrel. No matter how stunning the location.

So, as for the disappointment on this particular occasion, Charlie retains a healthy sense of perspective. Give him a couple of years and he'll very likely have got over it.

CHARLIE'S NOTEBOOK

There's just one small difficulty in catching salmon as they swim upriver. They don't eat. So the very basis of most rod and line fishing – to con a fish into swallowing what it thinks is food – is useless. The trick with salmon-fishing is to tempt the animal to fall off the wagon and break its diet. To trigger a response that bypasses its immediate lack of interest in food, and taps into some more fundamental stimulus. No salmon has yet filled out a questionnaire on the subject, but it seems likely that if one does snap at a fly, or 'spinner', it's down to one or both of two things. A deep-seated feeding instinct that it can't help itself acting on; or, as I personally believe, an aggressive one. To stir up these responses, the fly, or spinner, needs to be enticing, or irritating, or both. (A fly tends, Blowfish suggests, to trigger the feeding response; a spinner, which looks and behaves like a small annoying fish, the aggressive one.)

Whatever response it's hoping to stimulate, the artificial fly has to look and act like a real one. In hardcore fly-fishing circles, choosing the right fly, let alone tying it yourself, is often discussed in terms of hushed, masonic reverence. But there is, as so often where fishing's concerned, a counter-argument: just keep things simple. Rather than its intricate design, what's crucial is the depth at which you can keep the fly 'swimming', the speed at which you can make it travel; and the skill with which you can make it mimic the actions of a real fly. Get any of these factors wrong and the salmon will think you're just having a laugh, and pass you by.

BAHAMAS

THE LOCATION: LONG ISLAND, THE BAHAMAS

THE FISH: LIONFISH

Nassau

Long Island

A SERIES OF 'WANTED – DEAD OR ALIVE' posters has started to appear across the Bahamas, describing Public Enemy Number One in this part of the world. But it's not Jesse James, Pablo Escobar or El Chapo; here, the most dangerous threat is a 38cm long fish. The red lionfish and its partner in crime, the common lionfish, are devastating the ecosystem of the coral reefs all over this region, from North Carolina down to Venezuela. The problem is particularly acute here in the Bahamas. Not only is the lionfish destroying the natural environment, the local economies are suffering heavily as well.

Blowfish's challenge – to himself, Jay and Charlie – is twofold. He wants to try some extreme, and extremely fun, fishing techniques, and at the same time to try to come up with some stratagems to take the lionfish out. Not one by one, but on an industrial basis. The bounty? To help restore the natural order of the reefs, and that includes the livelihood of hundreds of local fishermen. But to have any chance of success, the battle against the lionfish needs to work on a global, not just a local, scale. A joined-up plan that makes a material change to both the ecology and the economy of the Bahamas – to tip the balance back in the indigenous species' favour.

With 340 days of sunshine a year, and temperatures only dropping below 4°C for a few days every three decades, it's no surprise that the Bahamas are one of the world's most glamorous holiday destinations, the very epitome of a tropical island paradise. Sequences for seven James Bond movies were filmed here, and it has also provided locations for the *Pirates of the Caribbean* series. But under the seductive turquoise and sapphire waters, just beyond the golden, butterscotch beaches, the tropical calm belies a storm. Under the sea there's a war going on.

Lionfish are native to the Indian and Pacific Oceans. The first documented sighting of this infamous party in waters where it didn't belong was off the coast of Miami in 1985, though it may have arrived several years earlier. Now lionfish are everywhere – the Western Atlantic, the Gulf of Mexico, the Caribbean. They've been spotted as far north as Rhode Island, as far south as Brazil. Anywhere, indeed, where the water is warm enough for their liking. Once settled in, they come on like a plague of underwater locusts, and lay waste to the living coral.

BLOWFISH:
'ONCE ONE OF THESE DUDES HAS MADE IT ON TO A REEF, THEY CAN REMOVE HALF OF ALL THE SPECIES IN JUST A SINGLE YEAR. THIS THING IS A MOUTH WITH FINS. AND IT HAS BEEN GRANTED DIPLOMATIC IMMUNITY.'

FACT FILE THE BAHAMAS

The Bahamas is a coral archipelago consisting of more than 700 islands.
Columbus first made landfall here on his world-changing voyage of 1492.
The Spanish didn't colonize the islands, but they did carry off the inhabitants
as slaves, a sign of the grim things to come in the New World. Most of the
population died of European germs, guns and steel. The islands were all but
abandoned, until British Puritans began to arrive in 1648. Then came the
'Pirates' Republic' (1706–18), as buccaneers took over the Bahamas and used
Nassau as a base for their dastardly depredations. They included the most
famous of them all, 'Blackbeard' (Edward Teach). The Bahamas became a
Crown Colony in 1718, as a crackdown on piracy got under way.

After the American War of Independence (1775–83), Americans still loyal
to the British were settled here. They brought with them their African slaves.
This shameful trade in human degradation was banned in British ships in
1807, and the USA forbade the importation – but not the exploitation – of
its victims the following year. After this, the Bahamas became a home for
freed, resettled and escaped slaves. Over 80% of the overall population
today is of African heritage.

It has to be said that the lionfish is a most attractive fish to look at.
Indeed, it's long been a popular choice for aquariums. And that, it seems, has
been our undoing, and the cause of a disastrous chain reaction. Although it's
possible they hitched a ride in the ballast tanks of ships to colonize new areas,
the popular theory is that lionfish were introduced into the seas near Florida
from aquariums. (Some of which were damaged by Hurricane Andrew in 1992.)
Which, if true, makes its arrival here one of the worst and most ill-advised man-
made ecological disasters we've perpetrated on the planet. Lionfish in these
waters are a classic and stark example of an 'invasive species' and the havoc
they can wreak if they're let loose where they shouldn't be given a foothold.
This beauty is a beast.

BLOWFISH:
'THEY'RE HERE ON A LONG-HAUL HOLIDAY, WITH AN OPEN BUFFET OF REEF FISH, AND IT LOOKS LIKE IT'S THE RESIDENTS OF THE BAHAMAS WHO ARE GOING TO BE FOOTING THE BILL.'

KNOW YOUR ENEMY

There are estimated to be 50 million lionfish in the Bahamas alone. And counting. A mature female lionfish lays eggs every three to five days, producing around 25–30,000 eggs with each spawn. In the course of a year she may produce over 2 million of them.

No wonder the lionfish here have acquired the nickname, 'The Pirates of the Caribbean'. Or, less glamorously, the 'rats of the sea'. No wonder too that the catch for the local fishermen – especially lobsters – has been more than decimated. Lionfish are causing an economic disaster here as well as a natural one.

Lionfish are voracious. Their mouths open as wide as their bodies. To accommodate their rapacious appetite they can expand their stomachs up to thirty times their normal size. They're not fussy feeders: they're known to prey on over fifty different species, including young barracudas, marlin, groupers, parrotfish, snapper, flounder, tuna, lobster, shrimp, crab, octopus, squid and seahorses. If it will fit into the lionfish's mouth, then it's on the menu. And that includes organisms that are absolutely vital for the health and survival of the living coral.

Coral reefs amount to less than 1% of the world's oceans by size but they contain 25% of the world's marine life. They easily rival rainforests in the intensity of their biodiversity. But for how much longer? Some ecologists estimate that around a quarter of the world's coral reefs may already have been damaged beyond the point of no return. And the tragedy is that the lionfish can't be put in the dock as the sole agent of the destruction of the coral in this part of the world. Over-fishing, boats and divers chipping off bits of the coral, pollution, and global warming: all have seriously weakened the reefs. The lionfish have moved in for the *coup de grâce*.

Once a reef is infested with them, the species slaughter begins. Reef fish don't just look pretty; some play a role in keeping the coral healthy by feeding on algae. But if these 'grazers' are wiped out, it's a slow death for the coral. As fast-growing green algae start to settle, they overwhelm the slow-growing colourful corals, choking them of light. The once-vibrant reef becomes a hairy green eyesore.

If the grazers could return, they would quickly strip the algae right back, leaving the door open for corals to re-colonize the area. But it can take hundreds of years for even a small reef to bloom into wondrous life and support the diversity these reefs are so famous for. And there's no chance this slow process will happen while the lionfish – the grim reefers – are still around.

The lionfish infestation is a perfect storm – every possible factor that could be in its favour is ticked off here in the Bahamas. Their biggest advantage is that they have no natural predators in the Western Atlantic or the Caribbean, thus giving them a free rein. Back in the Indo-Pacific, where the lionfish originally comes from, sharks are one of its main predators, but because the lionfish is such a new arrival in the Bahamas the sharks here haven't yet identified it as a suitable prey. So the first of the three prongs in Blowfish's plan will be to see if the culinary habits of the local sharks can be extended by putting lionfish on the menu. Or at least, as an *amuse-bouche*.

To introduce the sharks to a new form of prey, Blowfish will have to get more than close enough for comfort – in effect, he has to spoon-feed the lionfish to them. Liz Parkinson, a shark conservationist based in Nassau, the Bahamian capital, has dived with sharks thousands of times, and has the scars to prove it. She's come along to offer some local knowledge and help make sure that Blowfish doesn't get eaten himself. Caribbean reef sharks and nurse sharks aren't quite in the top league in terms of causing fatalities or serious injuries to man. But, with some of the female reef sharks coming in at around 3.5 metres long, and with the added danger of feeding the sharks himself, almost literally by hand, Blowfish will be wearing a chainmail suit, just in case.

Liz and Blowfish, kitted out and with dead lionfish as bait, head out into the deep waters where the sharks are most likely to gather. Blowfish is an expert scuba diver, and he's had plenty of experience of diving where sharks are in the water, but the sudden flurry around them is something else. Fifteen metres down, on the sea floor, it's a free-for-all. Unsynchronized swimming, an explosion of energy; there are around a dozen sharks swirling around them at any one moment. Their bodies sliding along those of Blowfish and Liz, in an underwater lambada; bumping into their heads, having a little experimental nibble at Blowfish's chainmail-protected hand. Suddenly, that suit of armour doesn't feel quite so impregnable.

The million-dollar question is, will the Bahamian sharks be willing to try a bit of lionfish? Blowfish spears one from his cache and edges it towards a reef shark, who snaps it up eagerly! All at once a feeding frenzy begins. Blowfish gets into the swing of things, stabbing lionfish towards every available customer. The sharks seem more than keen: the lionfish are going down a treat. Blowfish had been worried that the venomous spines might cause the sharks a problem, but they don't seem bothered by them at all.

Blowfish is delighted. The experiment shows that the native sharks seem perfectly happy with the taste of lionfish. In theory, once they know it can be eaten, they will continue to eat it. But when will that realization sink in? And how much irreversible damage will the lionfish have done in the meantime?

BLOWFISH:
'IF THEY REALLY WANT TO, THEY COULD TURN US INTO ... WELL,
I DON'T LIKE TO THINK WHAT THEY MIGHT TURN US INTO.'

How the lionfish plague affects the livelihoods of the Bahamians is brought home to Charlie, Blowfish and Jay when they visit Long Island, one of the most remote and beautiful in the Bahamas. With its dramatic cliffs and caves on the east coast, where it fights off the Atlantic, and its golden beaches on the lee shore, this was a popular harbour with the piratical Captain Kidd. And it's proved to be a real treasure island for the lionfish, who are terrorizing the indigenous population down on the reefs.

Charles Knowles has been fishing for lobster in Long Island since he was a boy. Now the lionfish is eating up the young lobsters, shrimp, crabs – the very catch the locals rely on: 80–90% of the men here make their living fishing. Charles takes the guys out to his lobster traps, known locally as 'condos'. It's a sobering sight: the twenty condos have yielded just two adult lobsters. That represents a week's effort, including regular checking of the traps. The pair are worth the princely sum of 24 dollars. Before the lionfish got to work, Charles would have expected to catch around six lobsters in each condo. So today's haul is around a sixtieth of what it might have been ten years ago.

BLOWFISH:
'SO THE LIONFISH COULD SHUT DOWN LONG ISLAND?'

CHARLES:
'COMPLETELY. IF WE DON'T STAY AFTER IT, IT WILL. WHAT WE'RE LOOKING AT NOW IS OUR FUTURE, OUR KIDS' FUTURE, OUR GRANDKIDS' FUTURE. WE WANT TO PROTECT THAT.'

If the lionfish invasion can't be stemmed, these islands might be headed for where they were in the sixteenth century. All but abandoned.

Catching the lionfish presents a whole raft of problems. Rod and line fishing, Charlie's forte, won't work because lionfish won't take bait. So far the only method that has proved halfway viable for catching the interlopers is spear-fishing. In the USA, 'lionfish derbies' have become a popular pastime since the danger posed by these ornery critters was first recognized. There are now dozens of these underwater rodeos, from the Florida Keys to Chesapeake Bay, with cash prizes offered for the diver spearing the biggest (or smallest) lionfish, or the largest number of them. But what everyone who has studied the problem agrees is that taking the lionfish out one by one by dedicated amateur divers is but a drop in the ocean.

And there's a considerable drawback in engaging with them at close quarters in any case: they can bring you a world of excruciating pain. The lionfish has between fifteen and eighteen venomous spines. They're not used to attack its prey; the spines are primarily a defence mechanism. But get near enough to it that it feels threatened – or let it get near enough to you that a sudden movement on your part can startle it – and it will stand its ground. The world's worst hangover can in no way compare to the pain a sting will cause … The venom won't be fatal, but it could put you out of action for up to a week. As Charles Knowles knows to his cost. 'You feel a fatigue like you're dizzy, like your eyes are going to roll back, like you want to vomit. You try to walk, you're going to fall.'

And not only is an attack extremely painful; the week or so you'll spend recovering is a week's earnings down the drain. Little wonder the fishermen here are happier fishing for something else. So the second prong of Blowfish's lionfish-slaying trident is to identify a more effective way of catching them, which can also help to prevent people from being stung.

Of course, he's not the first to put his mind to this. Environmentalists all over the affected seaboards have been doing so since the scale of the disaster became apparent. One obvious idea is to try to catch the lionfish in traps. To this end, Bob and Maria Hickerson, a team of Florida divers and lionfish hunters, have come down to the Bahamas to show the team a nifty prototype they've been developing. It works in a similar way to the long-established lobster trap. (In Florida some lobster fishermen have had success in catching lionfish, which inspired the idea.)

The big difference is that there is no bait. Instead, the idea is to leave the trap at the bottom of the reef, so that its insides gradually become encrusted with marine life. Then, the hope is that the lionfish might mistake it for a reef ledge, from which they like to hunt, and swim in. And here's the clever bit. If the fish enters the 'foyer', an electronic profiling device fitted within the trap determines whether it is a lionfish or not. If it gets through customs a gate opens and allows it to swim into the trap proper, while other fish are denied entry.

And so comes the day of reckoning. The trap is hauled up to the surface, all eyes eagerly searching for the rich catch of lionfish that will surely be inside. On closer examination the team are devastated to see that it contains absolutely nothing. The inventors will have to go back to the drawing board; but in the

trap's defence, it should be said that on this occasion, thanks to the logistics of the trip, it was only in the water for a relatively short amount of time. If it is going to work, it will need far longer underwater in order to transform it into a mini marine environment that might attract a lionfish.

Blowfish is more intrigued by the possibility of a trap aimed at juvenile lionfish, especially in mangrove swamps, which often serve as nurseries. Young lionfish are nervous, and here it's more likely that one might seek the shelter of such a trap. Culling the juveniles, of course, cuts the problem off at the source: kill adults and really, you're too late.

With any progress yet to come out of the traps, it's time to test out the last, and by far the most important element of Blowfish's campaign to smash the lionfish racket. The only way to beat them is to eat them. Only when lionfish become popular as food will commercial fishermen be incentivized to catch them. A swanky New York restaurant has tried to start the ball rolling, offering lionfish as an enticing – and reassuringly expensive – new delicacy. If it comes to be seen as a prize *poisson du jour* in fancy restaurants that's a bonus. It's the local market in the Bahamas that's by far the most vital one to crack; and that won't be easy.

Anyone who's been following the lionfish story thus far won't be surprised to learn that there's yet another factor in its favour. Among the Bahamians there's an understandable, but wholly mistaken belief that because they are venomous, lionfish are also poisonous. They're not, and shouting this fact from the clifftops is crucial if the lionfish are going to take their place on the islands' tables.

Venom is dangerous, even fatal, if it enters the bloodstream. But the flesh (as opposed to the spines) of a venomous fish is safe to eat. Poisonous fish, on the other hand, are dangerous, even fatal to eat. On this pivotal difference the battle against the lionfish may ultimately depend.

To see if the Long Islanders can be tempted to try them, the boys have arranged a beach banquet in which lionfish will be the main course. Invites have been issued, acceptances received. But as the hour for this gastronomic summit draws near, as is so often the case when you're throwing a dinner party, a vital ingredient is found to be missing. The lionfish. And they can't be ordered from Deliveroo. It's time to get back into the water. The lionfish hunt is on, in earnest.

Blowfish is putting his money on a 'slurp gun' – a device used by marine biologists to capture fish without harming them. (So this will be a new experience for it, as the opposite intention is the aim here.) The slurp gun is basically an underwater garbage chute powered by a toilet plunger. The *modus operandi* is pretty basic too. Flip the lid, place the opening next to the fish, take the plunge, and hey presto, the creature will be sucked up, the lid snapping shut behind it.

But Blowfish now comes up against yet another of the lionfish's armoury of tricks. Its natural behaviour is to insert itself into the nooks and crannies of a reef, hiding under ledges, and in general lurking around in places that make it extremely hard to winkle out. Even when Blowfish hammers off the lid, which protrudes so that it makes it impossible to get near enough to the coral (making it, as he remarks, 'a sawn-off slurp gun'), it's still nowhere near manoeuvrable enough, and the lionfish can keep well out of its way.

With the slurp gun, sawn-off or otherwise, failing to win its spurs, with rod and line fishing useless and with the use of nets prohibited, the only method open to the boys now is the tried and trusted one: spear-fishing. We know from the countless lionfish derbies that it works. But here in the Bahamas it will be doubly difficult. Strict regulations are in place to protect the coral and the indigenous sea creatures that co-exist with it. It's illegal here to fish using scuba equipment, to prevent too many fish being taken. And spear-fishing can only be done with a rather basic instrument, not the state of the art kit, complete with trigger, permissible in other parts of the world. The problem with some of these otherwise entirely sensible restrictions is that they have the unfortunate effect of protecting the lionfish as well as what it's feeding on. The local authorities here are in a double bind.

But although Jay and Charlie may only be packing a fairly basic weapon, a 'pole spear', they're not handling the lionfish with kid gloves. Theirs are coated with Kevlar, the stuff you get in a suit of body armour. This is surely a way forward: if the local fishermen can avoid getting stung, the lionfish won't pose such a threat to their safety, and their livelihoods.

But, having scouted the coral, Jay reports the big difficulty he and Charlie are going to face: the lionfish are jammed right into the reef, and extremely well camouflaged. Spearing them isn't going to be easy. At first, Charlie and Jay crack on in fine style. But their very success in spearing the lionfish spells danger. A shark has been attracted by the carnage. And a shark's sense of smell is so acute, Blowfish advises, that it can home in on a single drop of blood diluted in an Olympic-sized swimming pool. That's around 2,500 cubic metres.

Humans killing any type of fish in the vicinity of sharks really isn't a great idea, and moving to shallower waters where the sharks don't tend to go means the supply of lionfish dries up. Catching these predators one by one, while avoiding shark-infested waters, is clearly an ineffective way of waging war on the lionfish, but at least it's a start. And it's enough for supper, so the revels can begin.

The lionfish's culinary debut has arrived. The venomous spines have been carefully removed, the flesh has been grilled … what's the verdict? Well, the Great Bahamian BBQ is a winner. The lionfish are going down a storm. And as an added bonus, lionfish are good for you – they're fatty fish, extremely high in the universal panacea, Omega-3. This is excellent news all round, and extremely gratifying for Blowfish. If the lionfish can be sold as food, the fishermen hereabouts have a reason to catch it, and its numbers may – perhaps – be kept at bay.

There is an interesting and bizarre coda to the lionfish story. There is a theory being examined in the United States that the lionfish may be suffering an obesity crisis due to its unrestrained eating habits. Far more evidence needs to be gathered and tested before the theory is proven. If it does turn out that its very own version of an Elvis diet is in danger of killing it, the lionfish will learn the truth of the old adage soon enough: there's no such thing as a free lunch.

KENYA

THE LOCATION: **KENYA**

THE FISH: **THE NILE PERCH**

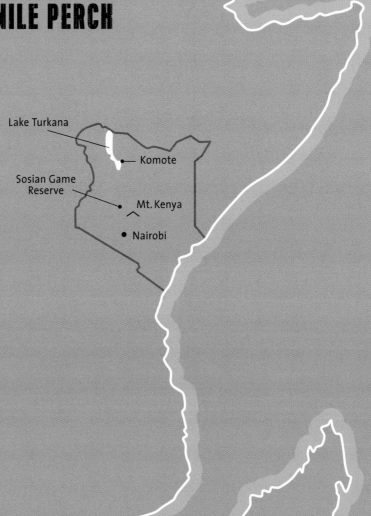

Lake Turkana

Komote

Sosian Game
Reserve

Mt. Kenya

Nairobi

THE CHALLENGE

IF BLOWFISH AND CHARLIE can rise to Jay's challenge in Kenya, fishing will be the icing on the cake. Just getting to the target location is going to be challenging enough: Jay wants to fish for the gigantic Nile perch in the remote Lake Turkana, in northern Kenya. It's the largest desert lake in the world. The surrounding terrain is one of the most inhospitable places on earth – baking hot, super-dry, and prone to lacerating rainstorms, racing sandstorms, and howling 50mph winds. There are not many places in the world where you can get both sunstroke and hypothermia on the same day. As a former Royal Marine Commando, Jay is used to the physical and mental rigours of surviving in extreme environments. Now it's Charlie and Blowfish's turn.

As the stork flies, the southern tip of the lake is only 300 miles from Nairobi. But to reach it will be a test of morale-sapping endurance for the whole team. It's not just the severe weather conditions: they will also be at the mercy of lions, elephants, leopards, hyenas and plenty of other dangerous customers if they break down along the way. And they can look forward to being stung by scorpions and bitten by vipers once they've arrived.

All this to catch a fish. But what a fish. The Nile perch are beasts, the largest freshwater fish in all of Africa, growing up to 2 metres and 200 kilos. Not only do they regard breaking fishing lines as child's play: they've been known to break rods too, and straighten hooks. So catching them won't be too easy. And there's another factor putting the job firmly in the Dangerous Sports category, one that Jay hasn't yet had the heart to reveal to Blowfish and Charlie. They'll be sharing the lake with one of the most deadly creatures known to man.

JAY:
'IT'S AN UNTOUCHED, UNSPOILED, UNWESTERNIZED ENVIRONMENT.
AND IT'S GOING TO BE A TEST OF ENDURANCE. ANYONE CAN FLY TO A
LOCATION AND CATCH A FISH; BUT YOU'VE GOT TO GO THROUGH SOME
PAIN TO GET THE REAL REWARDS.'

Mid-November. The boys fly into Nairobi, Kenya's capital and largest city, a crowded and busy metropolis home to some 3 million souls. Wasting no time, and eager to get the Nile perch contest under way, the team head out past the Nairobi suburbs and into the 'Central Highlands'. From the early years of the twentieth century until Kenya gained independence, in 1964, it was also known as the 'White Highlands', as most of the British colonialists lived here. You can see why they did: the scenery is lush and green, and the sense of scale is overwhelming. Big skies, big country, big animals. Lions, leopards, elephants, buffaloes and rhinos – the 'Big Five' safari treats – are joined by giraffes, zebras, antelope and wildebeest. In the beautiful lakes are flamingos, white pelicans, marabou storks and around 300 other species of birds.

The first port of call is the tiny Lake Rutundu, on the north-eastern slopes of the volcanic Mount Kenya, the country's tallest mountain, and the second highest in Africa after Mount Kilimanjaro, in neighbouring Tanzania. This should be the easy part of the journey. But the jeeps get stuck in the difficult terrain almost straight away, and there's an agonizing delay while the guide goes off for help.

This is a task which takes six hours, leaving the team and the camera crew marooned out in the open, in danger from marauding elephants and wildebeest, to say nothing of attack by leopards and hyenas. Welcome to Kenya!

When they finally arrive at Lake Rutundu, which is 12,000 feet above sea level, they find a beautifully seductive spot to go fishing, the silence broken only by the occasional cry of a fish eagle, or the snuffling peregrinations of a 'rock hyrax', or rock badger, set against dramatic views of snow-capped Mount Kenya, and the blue-green mountains beyond.

Here in Lake Rutundu, the boys will fish for trout; not, of course, a fish native to Africa, but one that is natural to Britain. The reason for this strange juxtaposition of fish and climate lies in Kenya's recent colonial history.

The British began settling in Kenya in 1905, as part of the European imperial powers' 'Scramble for Africa'. Three years later, to simulate the comforts of home, they decided to introduce brown, and later rainbow, trout into Lake Rutundu. The first brown trout here came from the famous fishery at Howietoun in Scotland, founded in 1881, which the boys visit in another chapter. Trout, largely thanks to the indomitable, some might say insane, efforts of the British, have been introduced into every continent except Antarctica.

Top of the list in the lake for Charlie, the fly-fishing fan, are the rainbow trout, native to the cold waters of the north Pacific. They survive in Lake Rutundu because its high altitude keeps the water cool.

We know there are plenty of trout in the lake, but after five hours, not one of the boys has had a hint of a bite. Lake Rutundu proves a perfect example of one of the most important rules in fishing: when in doubt, ask the locals. Charlie had been on the point of calling it a day when a Rutundu resident appeared and urged him not to throw in the towel just yet – early evening is the witching hour, the best time to catch a trout. This is because they tend to stay deep during the heat of the day, but become more active at dawn and dusk, when the water is cooler and they can move into the shallows to hunt. As usual, local knowledge turns out to be worth listening to: in almost complete darkness, Charlie finally hooks a trout.

And then … disaster, plucked from the jaws of triumph. Just as the fish is within an ace of being taken from the water, whoosh, and it's away. The guilty party here is Jay, who has forgotten to bring with him the net he's been packing all day.

But in truth, even with a net to hand, landing a fish that's still fighting for its life is not as trouble-free as it might look: take your eye off the ball even for an instant, and the fish can make its exit. All anglers have experienced it, more often than they'd care to remember. Except when exaggerating the size of the 'one that got away', of course.

But there's a happy ending – and something to eat for supper. Charlie hooks, and lands, a beautiful rainbow trout.

CHARLIE:
'THERE'S NOTHING MORE FRUSTRATING THAN LOSING A FISH WHEN IT'S IN TOUCHING DISTANCE. IT'S LIKE HAVING YOUR HAND ON A WINNING LOTTERY TICKET, AND THEN IT'S GONE.'

The next day the team drive north-west, to the Ewaso Narok River, which runs through the Sosian Game Ranch in the Laikipian plateau. This time they arrive without any major breakdowns – vehicular or mental – and they can set up in the river. The fish of the day here is the sharp-toothed catfish, a creature whose preferred habitat, Blowfish advises, is deep pools.

By a happy coincidence, 6 metres below the waterfall the boys are standing by, there is such a pool. After three death-defying leaps into the depths from the guys, they set up their rods and settle down to wait. From their side of the pool, Blowfish and Jay are both able to catch catfish. On the other bank though, Charlie isn't getting a whisker. His next move is radical. He decides to enlist the help of some of the most gigantic, and dangerous, animals in Africa. Further downstream there's a herd of hippopotamuses snorting away in the water.

FACT FILE **THE HIPPO**

The hippo, by some considerable distance, is the animal that causes the greatest loss of human life in the whole of Africa, if you discount the malaria-bearing mosquito. Hippo attacks are responsible for more human deaths than elephants and crocodiles put together.

In the water, hippos are extremely territorial, and extremely aggressive in defending that territory. An average fully-grown male weighs around 1,500 kilograms, and can be as much as double that size; a female not much less. They frequently attack boats, sometimes drowning the passengers. On land they are less territorial, but if spooked they will get back to the safety of the water as quickly as possible. And they *are* quick: they can reach 28mph over a short distance.

Anything in a hippo's way is barged aside, stomped on, or bitten. Their jaws are so large and powerful that they can, literally, bite a human in half. Their famous 'yawn' is actually a warning: it's the type of bellicose signal beloved of aggressive males in any species.

So when Charlie proposes that the boys fish from the bank next to some hippos downstream, casting their lines right into the herd, his plan isn't greeted with great enthusiasm. But there is plenty of sense behind it. In the cool of the evening, hippos come up on to dry land to eat grass. When they get back in the water, and start easing their bowels, their poo contains a grassy residue. And as they chew the grass, more falls into the water. All this attracts little fish. And where there are little fish – Charlie's logic is inexorable – you may well find bigger fish.

His reasoning pans out in fine style: he hooks a catfish from right under the noses of the hippos. This, for Charlie, is definitely one of the highlights of the trip.

CATFISH – THE SHARP END

Inside the sharp-toothed catfish's mouth are the objects that give it its name. To the naked eye, they don't actually look all that sharp – more like a worn-out toothbrush than a lethal weapon. Don't be fooled: these 'villiform' teeth act like Velcro. Row upon row of tiny, needle-sharp bristles (which is what 'villiform' means) ensure that once bitten, prey does not shy away.

What's really striking about catfish, though, is that if the water dries up, they can haul themselves out, and, using their powerful pectoral fins, 'walk' to a more favourable location.

Now, this does seem a bit mad. Surely, fish cannot survive out of water? Well, that's not entirely true. They can do if they're able to take in oxygen. And the catfish, along with some other species of fish, can breathe air! Fish also need to keep moist. The catfish can do this as well: it's evolved some quality mucus so that the tiniest amount of moisture, even morning dew, can keep it wet enough to protect it during its life on the open road.

Leaving Laikipia the next morning, Jay, Blowfish and Charlie plough north for the business end of the trip, the heart of Jay's challenge. As they enter the Northern Plains, and start approaching Lake Turkana, they're going to have to survive for three days in one of the most hostile environments on Earth. As Blowfish remarks, there are not many frontiers left on our planet. This is one, and it's dangerous. Settlements are few and far between, running out of water is unthinkable, and anyone injured would have to be air-lifted by helicopter to a hospital some distance away.

JAY:

'YOU'RE GOING TO BE TIRED, YOU'RE GOING TO BE COLD, YOU'RE GOING TO BE HOT. THERE MIGHT EVEN BE MOMENTS IN THIS JOURNEY WHERE YOU THINK, "YOU KNOW WHAT, I CAN'T GO ON ANY LONGER." THIS IS ABOUT SURVIVAL. WE'VE JUST GOT TO CRACK ON THROUGH, WORK AS A TEAM, AND WE WILL GET THERE.'

The excursion into the arid, rocky plains proves every bit as nerve-racking as the boys had feared. It's like motoring across Mars. After two gruelling and bone-shaking days of driving, involving eight-hour detours, dodging flash floods and torrential rain, running out of petrol and almost losing one of the 4x4s, it seems like a miracle. There it is, Lake Turkana, an oasis before them. The boys can see why it's sometimes called the 'Jade Sea'. Not only is it a beguiling blue and green; at over 6,400 square kilometres, it looks more like an ocean.

Around 9,000 years ago, the water level of this lake, and others nearby, was far higher. These waters fed into the White Nile. This is what allowed the Nile perch to find their way into Lake Turkana. Around 4,000 years ago, the water levels subsided, leaving the lake cut off from the mighty river. Until 1975 it was called Lake Rudolf, after an Austrian prince. Its present name derives from the most populous tribe who live along its shore, the Turkana people.

LAKE TURKANA

Because it has no outflows, and because of the evaporation caused by the extreme heat of this latitude, Lake Turkana is brackish and has been shrinking for several millennia. As the water reduces it gets progressively more alkaline: Lake Turkana is the largest 'alkaline lake' in the world.

As the pH of the water rises, simple biological processes become harder for the fish to control. The soft, delicate tissues of the gills have to balance salt uptake, waste excretion and the 'gas exchange' of oxygen and carbon dioxide with the surrounding environment. Here in Lake Turkana the fish are having to do all of this while swimming in bleach.

And remember, the fish species in Lake Turkana are also found all over this part of Africa; they have not evolved to survive in this lake alone. That they've adapted to do so at all is remarkable; that they've done so in such a relatively short period of time is truly extraordinary.

Lake Turkana may be inaccessible today, but millions of years ago it was the cradle of human existence. Beginning in the 1960s, paleo-anthropologists have turned up fossils of *Australopithecus anamensis*, a distant ancestor of *Homo sapiens*, that are around 4.2 million years old. They were found in Koobi Fora, on the north-eastern shore of the lake.

On this hallowed ground, then, how are our intrepid team of finely-tuned *Homo sapiens* going to shape up as they pit their wits against the Nile perch? Once again, the first item on the agenda is local knowledge. Charlie, Blowfish and Jay meet up with some of the Turkana people. It's a hospitable reception, a welcome change from that afforded by the desert, although Blowfish's mohawk causes some initial confusion and a good deal of hilarity: Turkana girls have their hair cut in exactly the same style to signal the onset of sexual maturity.

The fishing spot the Turkana people have selected for the battle is 'Bird Island', a tiny teardrop of land west of Komote, where the team have made base camp. Here, the local hosts assure the boys, Nile perch are waiting to be caught. It's all looking fairly straightforward, until Jay reveals one small wrinkle that he hasn't yet mentioned. Lake Turkana has a large population of another animal, which, like the perch, made its way into the lake thousands of years ago when its waters joined those of the Nile. The Nile crocodile. Here in the lake is the greatest number of them in all Africa.

Blowfish and Charlie receive this news with something less than stoical resignation. They're both fully in sympathy with Jay's obsessive desire to catch a Nile perch. But having risked their lives and their sanity to get here in the first place, asking them now to risk being eaten by crocodiles seems to take things a bit too far. Especially when their guide – himself the lucky survivor of a crocodile attack – outlines the next day's programme, which involves swimming the 500 metres to Bird Island, past the crocodiles. This is shaping up to be the most terrifying swim of their lives.

To get used to fishing on the lake, Blowfish, Charlie and Jay are going to start off by going after the tilapia, the Nile perch's main prey. They're easier to catch than their predators, but this won't be a breeze. By eleven in the morning it's already a ferocious 37°C.

Cautiously – *very* cautiously – the team swim out to the fishing grounds. And now Jay leads from the back rather than the front. Perhaps feeling a little bit guilty that his fishing party might go down with all hands, he's selflessly bringing up the rear – the crocodiles will seize him first. Having reached the island without mishap, the team fish for tilapia with the most traditional of methods – hand-lining, with a line and hook wrapped around a wooden spool and thrown out into the water. It's a success. Tilapia are caught, and the crocodiles have been conspicuous only by their much-appreciated absence. One reason for that, though, is because local knowledge has once again come into play: the crocodiles have learned to stay away from the vigorously defended Turkana fishing spots. By and large, that is – they are still a real threat.

Then, come evening, back at camp, the famously temperamental elements of Lake Turkana take a hand. Charlie, Jay and Blowfish see that the birds above the lake are flying away from the area. A storm is brewing; birds can sense the change in atmospheric pressure that means one is on its way. The guides, too, are so in tune with the ways of the weather that they are able to read the signs long before their visitors.

Storms are frequent and unpredictable here because the lake heats and cools more quickly than the land, the difference in air pressure creating furious rain and winds. This storm hurls down hailstones that sting like ball-bearings. The Turkana fishermen avoid venturing into the lake in such a storm – the waves can become huge, and dangerous. In addition, because of the flat desert terrain that

surrounds the lake, there's nothing to stop even the puniest gust of wind racing along to its shores, super-sizing into a full-on sandstorm as it goes, and arriving at the shore now laden with dust and sand, what the Turkana people call the 'yellow wind'. Visibility is virtually zero, and the raging sand can skin you alive.

After a night spent hiding from the elements, the team head into the lake for the penultimate day of fishing for the Nile perch. Jay has deployed an inflatable paddleboard, while Blowfish is on a raft he's borrowed from the locals, his own self-constructed version having proved to be more useful as a submarine. Charlie has elected to fish with his rod and line on a tiny island nearer the shore.

After six hours of catching precisely nothing, Jay finally gets a bite. It's certainly a Nile perch: Blowfish sees it jump out of the water, and it's a monster: 100 kilos, Jay reckons. It's so strong that it pulls him and his paddleboard along with it as it puts up a ferocious fight. And then, just as record-breaking figures are swimming before Jay's eyes, it gets away! Jay is bitterly disappointed, but also impressed by his opponent's cunning, in using the paddleboard as a buffer to reduce tension on the line, allowing it to slip the hook.

The last day arrives, and the team spend yet more time fruitlessly waiting for a bite. Finally, the gods relent, and Jay, at last, hooks his prize. A Nile perch. It's hardly a giant, at 16–18 kilos, but if we translate all the effort and heartache it's cost Jay, Charlie and Blowfish into poundage, it's worth its weight in gold.

JAY:

'AFTER EVERYTHING WE'VE BEEN THROUGH, THIS LITTLE BEAUTY MIGHT JUST BE MY BEST FISH EVER.'

THAILAND

THE LOCATION: THAILAND

THE FISH: GIANT MORAY EEL

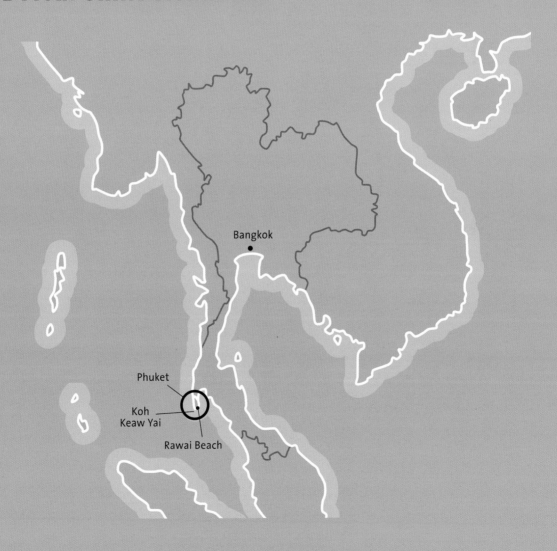

Bangkok

Phuket

Koh
Keaw Yai

Rawai Beach

CORNWALL-BRED JAY is a marine animal. He started fishing at six, but angling with rod and line proved far too passive an activity for his restless nature. Spear-fishing quickly became his passion; rather than wait for the fish to come to him, he prefers to go to them. Not with the help of a scuba suit, but using only what nature endowed him with – a set of lungs. One of Jay's long-standing dreams is to learn from the legendary 'Sea Gypsies' of Phuket, Thailand, the most awe-inspiring spear-fishers on the planet.

The Urak Lawoi start diving at the age of eight. They can see better in water than on land, and they can suffer from land-legs, rather than sea-legs, so habituated are they to an aquatic existence. They can dive to a depth of 40 metres and hold their breath for six minutes at a time. So how will Jay measure up to the masters? His best time so far is four minutes twenty.

The prize catch of the Sea Gypsies is one of the most fearsome fish in all the seas: the giant Moray eel. It can grow up to 3 metres in length and 30 kilos in weight; with its industrial-strength jaws and lethal teeth it's perfectly capable of ripping off fingers and thumbs. In severe cases, lower arms have had to be amputated after a Moray attack. Its appearance alone is the stuff of nightmares, its habitual expression of implacable aggression terrifying enough to drive a sliver of fear into the steeliest diver's heart – should he get close enough to witness it at first hand.

Which is exactly what Jay is proposing the team should do. His challenge to Blowfish and Charlie is not only to master the art of the free dive, but to lay hands on this most menacing monster of the deep. Without ending up in A&E.

It's December. Jay, Charlie and Blowfish have flown in to Phuket. It's a good time to be here, with average daytime temperatures around 27°C and almost guaranteed sunshine. Thailand has of course become a major leisure destination in recent decades, most particularly because of its blindingly white, sandy beaches. Alex Garland's best-selling novel, later a film, *The Beach,* portrays the quasi-mystical quest by Western backpackers for the ultimate unspoiled Thailand paradise.

As always, global tourism is a double-edged sword, creating jobs for the Thais, but westernizing the country's culture. Many beaches are fringed with international hotels and luxury resorts. It's regularly tipped by guidebooks as a 'surfers' paradise'. But for the more curious visitor, there are rainforests, jungles, mountains, ancient ruins and Buddhist temples to explore and to marvel at. There's a huge variety of wildlife, including gibbons, macaques and Asiatic black bears. In the water, giant freshwater stingray, giant carp and giant catfish as well as the giant Moray eel are worth taking the trip for. Phuket's coral reefs, and the rich diversity of life they support, make it a big favourite with dive-fans. And that's why the boys are here, in search of one of the most charismatic of marine creatures.

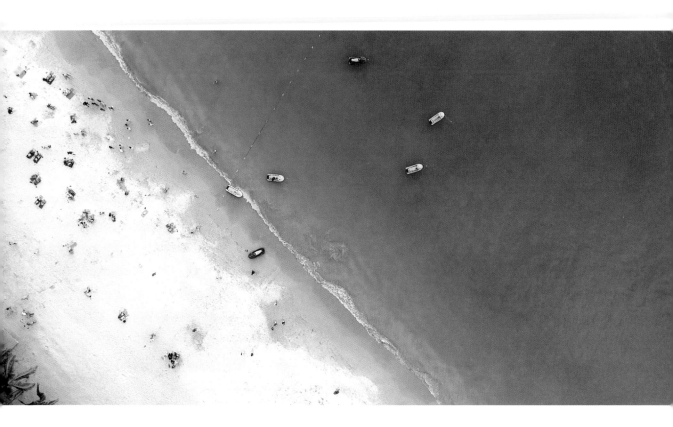

There are around 200 species of Moray eel. They're found all over the Indo-Pacific, in lagoons and coral reefs. They hunt at night, snapping up smaller fish and crustaceans. As Blowfish remarks to Charlie and Jay, large predators like the Moray are the heartbeat of a reef. Not only do they help maintain a healthy balance of predator and prey, they also protect the health of the reef fish. If there's a sick parrotfish, say, the Moray eel will be the first to kill and eat it. So whatever disease it's carrying dies with the fish, and it doesn't have the chance to spread the pathogens to the rest of the population. On the other hand, there is a considerable health risk to reef-visiting humans. You're more likely to be bitten by a giant Moray eel than by a shark.

As with all marine creatures, though, attacks on humans are comparatively rare. Giant Morays are actually rather shy and retiring creatures, who would much rather avoid humans than come into conflict with them. And when they do attack, it's almost invariably in self-defence; especially if their territories are being encroached upon, or they're feeding.

To get acclimatized, Jay, Charlie and Blowfish quickly leave the siren call of the beaches and head for the open sea. To the south and east of the large island of Phuket is a whole constellation of smaller islands and islets, some so tiny that they're only pinpricks on the map. The boys are being taken to Koh Keaw Yai, or 'Green Island', with the aim of testing the overall health of the seas in this area. If the number of smaller marine animals has been reduced – by over-fishing, pollution, global warming, or the devastating 2004 tsunami – then the creatures that subsist on them, including the giant Moray eel, simply won't be here.

The particular predator Charlie, Jay and Blowfish are in search of is the Lewis Hamilton of the Indian, Pacific and Atlantic oceans, the sailfish. If these speed merchants are around, it indicates a ready supply of smaller fish. After hours of waiting, a worrying delay that could indicate that the health of the waters is in decline, they finally get a bite – and a ten-minute, desperate struggle to reel it in. The sailfish, despite its size, is not just quick: it's extremely powerful.

Sailfish are not good to eat, so putting it back is the only thing to do. Before it's released, though, it's fitted with a basic tag, noting the time and place it was caught plus its vital statistics. Tagging has to be done quickly, to minimize trauma to the fish. And it is: this one is tagged and released within forty seconds of leaving the water.

SAILFISH

The sailfish, so named for its huge, flowing, dark blue dorsal fin, has been clocked at nearly 70mph. It's the fastest fish in the ocean. Its powerful body muscles, cleverly entwined around the 'caudal peduncle' – the narrow part of the fish's body to which the tailfin is attached – are what allow it to shift. The dorsal fin, which runs the whole length of its back, is used for control, for signalling and for corralling prey.

Its upper jaw is in the form of a long spear, or 'bill'. Together with swordfish and marlin, sailfish make up the group known as 'billfishes'. The sailfish uses its bill just the way a knight on horseback used a lance in a medieval tourney. Diving through shoals of potential prey, it flicks it rapidly at anything that takes its fancy: anchovies, sardines, triggerfish, ribbonfish, jacks and other marine delicacies. Anything caught by this deadly sideswipe is left dazed and confused, easy pickings for the hunter as it now doubles back to gobble up its dinner.

The fact that they've caught a sailfish at all gives the team some hope, at least, that their ultimate target, the giant Moray, will also be quietly going about its business in these waters. To limber up for the battle ahead, the next day Charlie, Blowfish and Jay head for a far less hospitable environment than the famous Phuket beaches: the mangrove swamps – salty, brackish water near the coast, within which only plants and animals that can cope with the high levels of salinity can survive.

The boys are aiming to get to grips with a creature that, like the hippos of their Kenya trip, has a fatal attraction to mud, glorious mud. And while it's not going to bite you into several pieces, like the hippo, it can certainly do some damage: they're after the giant mud crab, highly regarded here as food.

THE GIANT MUD CRAB

Like the giant Moray eel, the giant mud crab is nocturnal. Like the giant Moray, it's hard to find, and dangerous to try to catch. In the daytime it secretes itself in well-hidden nooks, crannies and crevices, into which it is ill-advised to venture an exploratory hand.

Recently a giant mud crab weighing nearly 3 kilos and measuring 60cm from claw to claw was found here in the Phuket mangroves – a proper Crabzilla. It's a mighty hunter: 'chemosensory' patches on its feet allow it to taste the tracks of its prey, which, if found, will finish up on the wrong end of its murderous claws.

The humble crab, in all its forms, is the Swiss Army knife of the animal world. It can eat food of any size, from the flesh of freshly-killed prey down to the slimiest of algae. The crab doesn't masticate: instead it can take a whole side of a fish, shred it into big chunks with its main claw, and cut it into ever-smaller chunks with a succession of slicing and dicing maxillas and mandibles. Imagine an abattoir attached to the front of your face! Finally, these meaty morsels reach the mouth, where a process called the 'gastric mill' grinds up whatever's left into a tasty paste.

Catching crabs here isn't going to be easy, especially in the full heat of the day. As the boys pitch up, it's a punishing 37°C. And while the Englishmen might be out in the midday sun, the crabs are not mad enough to join them. By now they will have dug themselves deep into the mud, to form a well-shielded lair. To add to the fun, the mangrove is also home to venomous snakes, spiders, scorpions, crocodiles and juvenile reef sharks, all riding shotgun nearby.

Blowfish, though, is in his element, literally, fishing with his bare hands. He is the first to catch a crab; his superior handling skills come to the fore, since experience has taught him to be wise to the crab's tricks as it tries to give him a retributory nip with one of its sharp, powerful pincers. Jay and Charlie, not being marine biologists, aren't sorry to leave the fetid mangrove swamp, despite their both having caught crabs. This isn't really their idea of fishing.

The mud crab jamboree has given the team an insight into how tricky it will be to find the equally elusive giant Moray eel deep in its own hiding place. And now it's time to meet the Sea Gypsies, to attempt just that.

As ever, with any form of fishing in a new environment, the best way of getting on the inside track is to learn from the pros. The Sea Gypsies have been catching giant Moray eel for hundreds of generations, as the fish is a delicacy here, though something of an acquired taste where the Western palate is concerned. What's more, it can be dangerous to eat, thanks to ciguatera, a toxin that affects the flesh of some reef fish. Nonetheless, giant Morays are sold at the local markets (if they are under 1.5 metres in length they are judged safe to consume) and remain the most prized of the Sea Gypsies' prey.

FACT FILE **SEA GYPSIES**

The term 'Sea Gypsy' is loosely applied to several ancient nomadic tribes who live by spear-fishing in south-east Asia. Jay, Charlie and Blowfish are going to be diving with the Urak Lawoi, whom they'll be joining near Rawai Beach, on the south-east coast of Phuket.

For millennia the Sea Gypsies have roamed all over this region in small boats, diving with spears of their own making. Like gypsies in Europe, they are perennial outsiders, fiercely protective of their way of life. But that is increasingly under threat. Petroleum was found off the coast of Myanmar (Burma, as was) in the 1990s, and this factor, allied to a suppression of supposedly suspect ethnic groups conducted by the military regime, resulted in the nomadic Sea Gypsies being forcibly 'settled'. For a whole raft of reasons, mostly to do with tourism, the government of Thailand is also eager to rid their western coast of these aquatic nomads and place them in something akin to reservations. The Sea Gypsies, are, it seems, fighting a losing battle against 'progress'.

The giant Moray is not so gigantic when it comes to the brain department, as Blowfish points out – it's the size of a peanut. This is not to cast aspersions on its IQ. In the only known example of different species of fish joining forces to hunt prey, the Moray eel sometimes teams up with the 'Roving Coralgrouper'. The eel's role in this deadly duo is to use its ability to swim into confined spaces to drive smaller fish out into the open water. Blowfish points out the smallness of the giant Moray's brain because it means that the 'kill shot' has to be taken at the first opportunity, with no room for error. As Jay puts it: 'The Moray eel's not a fish to mess around: shoot and miss and it will take your hand off.'

FACT FILE FREE-DIVING

The diving suit was invented by Leonardo da Vinci, in as much as he drew a sketch for one. The first workable diving suits, immensely cumbersome as well as dangerous and inefficient, came into being in the early eighteenth century and were used successfully in the salvage (or plunder) of wrecks. The modern diving apparatus, the 'Aqua-Lung', or Scuba (Self Contained Underwater Breathing Apparatus), was co-invented in the early 1940s by the important pioneer of marine biology and conservation, Jacques Cousteau. His many odysseys among the coral reefs aboard the yacht *Calypso*, aided by his son Yves, were a staple on cinema and television screens all over the globe during the 1950s, 60s and 70s.

For aeons before all this, of course, what's now called 'free-diving' was the only sort of diving: just you, a pair of lungs and the deep blue sea. In recent decades, boosted by Luc Besson's film *The Big Blue* in 1988, an extreme form of free-diving has become a dangerous obsession for some endurance-junkie thrill-seekers who will use any method to go as deep as they can in search of new records. All kinds of performance-enhancing tricks are used, often involving the intake of pure oxygen, which allows the diver to hold their breath for longer. The current free-diving record is an astounding 214 metres.

JAY ON SPEAR-FISHING:

'IT'S ABOUT GETTING IN THE WATER AND ADAPTING, BECOMING LIKE A FISH, THINKING LIKE A FISH. AFTER A WHILE IT GETS TO BE AN ORGANIC PROCESS. YOU KNOW WHERE THE FISH ARE GOING TO BE – IT'S USING YOUR HUNTER-GATHERER INSTINCTS.

NOTHING GOES TO WASTE. I'LL ONLY SHOOT WHAT I'M GOING TO EAT, OR IT'S JUST AN ABSOLUTE WASTE. WHEN I FINISH I ALWAYS GUT THE FISH AND THROW THE HEAD AND GUTS BACK IN, AS FOOD FOR OTHER CREATURES. SO I'VE STOLEN SOMETHING FROM THE OCEAN, BUT I'M GIVING SOMETHING BACK.

SPEAR-FISHING AND FREE-DIVING ARE TWO DIFFERENT SPORTS. I'M NOT INTERESTED IN DIVING 100 METRES – IT'S PITCH BLACK! I ONLY DIVE TO WHATEVER DEPTH I NEED TO DO TO HUNT THE FISH I'M AFTER. IF I SEE A BASS THAT'S 3 METRES UNDERWATER, I DIVE 3 METRES.'

JAY:

'I HADN'T REALIZED HOW DANGEROUS THE NEEDLEFISH ARE. THEY CAN SWIM INTO YOU LIKE DARTS. IF YOU MISS THE TARGET THEY SCATTER IN THE WATER, THAT'S HOW PEOPLE GET STABBED BY THEM, WHEN THE NEEDLEFISH PANIC.'

Jay's been spear-fishing since he was twelve. But before letting a Cornishman loose in their favoured fishing spots, the Urak Lawoi want to assess his chances of survival. To put his marksmanship to the test, they take Jay out to spear for needlefish. As the name implies, these are Size Zero models, long and skinny. The kill shot, right behind the gills, has to be absolutely on the money. The target is less than 5cm in diameter – behind the gill plate through which the fish gets its oxygen.

Jay passes with flying colours, and spears one right through the brain. That's good news on two counts. In the first place, it reassures his guides that he can walk the walk. In the second, what they hadn't told him is that the needlefish, like the Moray, comes after you if you shoot and miss.

Sad to say, Jay's long-awaited Indian Ocean dive was not all he'd been hoping for; there weren't anything like the number of large fish he'd expected. Years and years of over-fishing here have taken their toll. The Sea Gypsies, to make their living, now have to dive down to 60 metres, far further than their traditions – and traditional methods – allow. They have had to resort to using air supplied by compressor units mounted on boats above them, rather than just the prodigious capacity of their lungs.

But it's time for the team to gear up for Jay's challenge. To show them what they're up against, Blowfish sets up a makeshift laboratory bench and dissects a giant Moray eel head he's bought in a local market. It's not a pretty sight.

GIANT MORAY EEL

The giant Moray eel has truly awesome jaws. In the first place its teeth face backwards. So anything that finds its way into that fearsome-looking gullet is going to find it doubly difficult to find its way out again. And that's only the half of it. The Moray eel has *two* sets of jaws. The larger set where you can see it; the smaller, known to biologists as the pharyngeal jaws, hidden deep in its throat. The larger jaws impale the victim on rows of razor-sharp teeth like broken shards of glass. Then the smaller set of jaws shoots forward from the back of the throat to kill or wound the fish, and start ripping out large chunks of flesh. If the quarry does manage to get away, the eel will still be able to hang on to something. And thanks to the anticoagulant properties of the Moray's oral mucus, the wounded victim's cuts will not heal. Most likely it will bleed to death and then the Moray can use its excellent sense of smell to track down the corpse and finish off the job.

Unlike its gruesome facial appearance, the giant Moray eel's movement through the water is extremely graceful. It's sinuous, smooth, and delicate – like a flag being blown in a gentle breeze. But it's also powerful. When it wants to motor, it extends its dorsal, anal and caudal fins and flattens its body, becoming more like a blade than a cylinder. Think of a torpedo with teeth – not something you'd want to join for an underwater tango.

To find out how badly wrong things can go, Jay, Blowfish and Charlie meet a British ex-pat, Matt Butcher, who has spent sixteen years skippering boats in these waters. He has first-hand experience of a giant Moray eel attack: one actually bit his thumb clean off. It's now been surgically replaced by one of his toes, thanks to a miracle of medical science. The accident, he cheerfully admits, occurred when he was feeding the animal a string of sausages.

The aim of this underwater Punch & Judy show is to make a living. It's in the interests of people operating sub-aqua tours to keep the customer satisfied, and that means tempting out the star turns, such as the giant Moray.

Now, you might think that Blowfish, as a marine biologist, might not entirely approve of this sort of activity, but his view is that it could have a benefit further down the line. If seeing a giant Moray close up makes the punters better appreciate, or perhaps even fall in love with, the beauty and marvellous complexity of the underwater world, that can only add recruits to the 'hearts and minds' campaign to save it from damage or destruction.

There is, it's fair to say, an undoubted risk attached to feeding sausages to a giant Moray eel. Not least because it isn't blessed with particularly good eyesight, so sausages, thumbs and fingers are not that easy for it to tell apart. Blowfish's way of explaining the perils of feeding dangerous fish is to consider that a predator will usually go into attack mode only when a number of boxes have been ticked – which, taken together, switch on a green light and klaxon indicating 'food'. If humans regularly make themselves part of this suite of ideas, and become indelibly associated with feeding opportunities in the piscine mind, mistakes can be made and disaster can follow, as Matt Butcher found out.

And so, the day of reckoning. In the company of the Urak Lawoi spear-fishers, Jay puts on his snorkel and dives for the deep. He has the ultimate challenge of executing the golden shot, while Charlie and Blowfish, also free-diving, are assigned scouting and look-out duties.

As ever with impossible fishing, nothing happens quickly. After hours and hours in the water, no sign of a giant Moray is to be found. The team have to move further out to sea.

And then the sharp-eyed Blowfish spots one hiding in a crevice in the reef, with its characteristic expression of inscrutable menace as it slowly opens

and shuts its dinosaur-like jaws. Its head alone is poking out from a fissure in the coral, where, thanks to its camouflage, it's nearly invisible. Now it's up to Jay. He has one chance, remember: miss the brain and one very angry eel is going to shoot out like a bullet from a gun to exact its revenge.

Jay gets closer and closer. The giant Moray makes no move. Jay inches closer still – the kill shot is on. The eel still doesn't flinch; it seems oblivious, completely unaware that its demise is only a heartbeat away. But then ... with the Moray's brain only inches from the tip of his spear, Jay can't bring himself to shoot. He swims back up to the surface.

In Blowfish's feeding model, once a predator has ticked various boxes it goes in for the kill. Jay has ticked all the boxes and made a personal decision *not* to go in for the kill.

JAY:

'THIS IS THE FIRST TIME I'D SEEN A GIANT MORAY IN REAL LIFE. IT WASN'T WHAT I WAS EXPECTING. IT LOOKED SO CALM AND PEACEFUL IN ITS NATURAL HABITAT. SHOOTING A STATIC TARGET, SUCH A BEAUTIFUL FISH, AT POINT BLANK RANGE JUST DIDN'T FEEL RIGHT.'

BLOWFISH:

'NOT ONLY HAVE YOU MADE THAT MORAY EEL'S DAY, JAY, YOU'VE MADE MINE AS WELL. I AM SO PROUD OF YOU, MATE, WELL DONE.'

And one lucky giant Moray eel will live to see another day.

PATAGONIA

THE LOCATION: PATAGONIA
THE FISH: PATAGONIAN TOOTHFISH

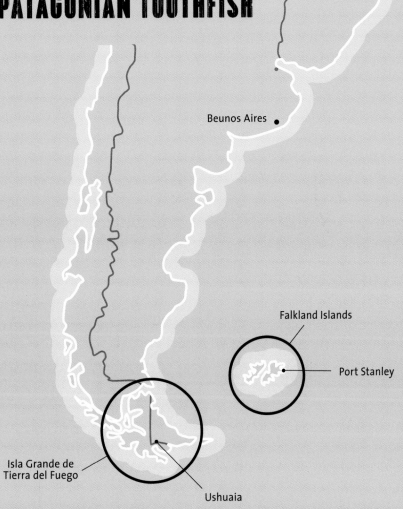

Beunos Aires

Falkland Islands

Port Stanley

Isla Grande de
Tierra del Fuego

Ushuaia

CHARLIE HAS BROUGHT Jay and Blowfish to the end of the world in search of fish. They're on the island of Tierra del Fuego, the land of fire, at the southern tip of Patagonia. Here are some of the most dangerous seas on the planet, surrounding the fearsome barrier of Cape Horn. The Magellan Strait, which separates Tierra del Fuego from the mainland, is named after the mastermind of the first ever circumnavigation of the globe – a voyage that lasted from 1519 to 1522. This challenge, Charlie hopes, won't take quite as long, or involve quite as many casualties. One of whom was Ferdinand Magellan himself.

They've journeyed the 7,500 miles to Tierra del Fuego in search of 'white gold': the fabled Patagonian toothfish. Having worked as a chef before becoming an airline pilot, Charlie has heard of this legendarily toothsome item through the kitchen grapevine, but has never tasted, let alone caught one. Pound for pound, it's the most expensive fish you can eat. Not only is it regarded as a must-have item by wealthy gastronomes and food-obsessives, in the same bracket as *foie gras* or caviar, it's also incredibly difficult to catch. The Patagonian toothfish lives well over a kilometre deep in violent, storm-tossed seas. Its rarity and succulence mean it can sell for up to $150 a kilo. Little wonder there's a whole commercial fishing industry – legal and otherwise – that ship out daily in search of it. Just as Magellan wrote his name into the record books five centuries ago, Charlie now challenges the team to do the same. No amateur has ever caught a Patagonian toothfish.

As they arrive in Tierra del Fuego by helicopter, a tremendous vista unfolds before Charlie, Blowfish and Jay – huge and impressive green forests and white mountains. Magellan, seeing the fires lit by the indigenous peoples here when he first saw the island in 1520, originally called it 'Tierra del Humo', Land of Smoke. It was his sponsor, the Holy Roman Emperor, Charles V, who renamed it, perhaps thinking 'Land of Fire' more poetic. It does not disappoint, with its gaunt beauty, wild in tooth and claw: crashing breakers, sea mists, lakes, rivers, mountains (the Andes run out of steam here), forests and tundra.

The Argentinian territory of Tierra del Fuego is the Isla Grande – not just a big island, but the biggest in South America. In 1833 Charles Darwin sailed past its southern coast in HMS *Beagle*, in one of the most significant journeys in scientific history. Here in the deepest south, the temperatures can drop to −21°C.

To acclimatize to the punishing climate, Charlie takes Blowfish and Jay to a nearby lake to fish for trout. There are big fish here, and only one problem – the lake is frozen. The boys will have to come up with a nifty method of fishing under the ice. And Charlie has such a plan.

The idea is to fish with two rods on opposite sides of the lake, their lines tied together to make one big line, submerged under the ice. The boys go to the shallow end where the water has melted, Charlie on one side, Blowfish and Jay on the other. Charlie casts to the other bank, the two lines are joined together, and the resulting super-line, with a spinner at its junction, is manoeuvred below the icy shield. By rocking, rolling and reeling in turn, the spinner can be made to move back and forth, surely exciting the trout's proud hunting instincts.

But it's not so easy to fish in this winter wonderland. The ice may look smooth and flat on top, but underneath it's full of ridges – and there are plenty of submerged logs and rocks to snag the line. What's more, the team have no choice but to shout to each other across the water – not the kind of watercraft the manuals recommend. After several hours there are still no bites, and it's also bitterly cold – a full-scale blizzard has whipped up. This just isn't working for the boys, so they head back to the hotel to recuperate.

The boys are convinced that the two-line method *could* have been made to work; but there's no time to try again. They've caught trout before; here in Patagonia all eyes are on the main prize, the toothfish.

PATAGONIA

Patagonia, of which Tierra del Fuego is the southern spur, is shared by Argentina and Chile. But it's not so much a region as a state of mind. Its borders have never really been agreed upon; it's what it decides to be at any one moment. The territory has long held a fascination for outsiders – as evidenced in Bruce Chatwin's marvellous book *In Patagonia*, where he describes meeting the descendants of the hardy Welsh, Scottish, German and Boer communities who put down roots here in the nineteenth century. More immigrants – from as far away as California and Australia – were drawn by a gold rush in Tierra del Fuego at the end of the century. It wasn't just honest toil that inspired its visitors, though: in 1904 Butch Cassidy and the Sundance Kid turned up to rob one of Patagonia's leading banks.

Patagonia is a land of contrasts: from arid steppes to massive glaciers, from pampas grass and nomadic gauchos to vibrant marine fauna – southern right whales, elephant seals and Magellanic penguins. Depending on who's counting, there's roughly 800,000 square kilometres of Patagonia, with only one or two people per square kilometre – making it one of the most sparsely populated regions in the world, and one of its last genuine wildernesses.

THE PATAGONIAN TOOTHFISH

The Patagonian toothfish can be found in cool temperate and sub-Antarctic waters throughout the southern hemisphere. It can live for up to fifty years, and can grow to over 100kg and more than 2 metres – though somewhere around half this weight is more normal for most adults. They like the cold – operating in water temperatures between 1 and 4°C.

You'll find these guys at the bottom of the sea, sometimes at depths of nearly 4,000 metres. The toothfish isn't one for swimming; 'benthic' animals (those that live at the bottom of the ocean) like the toothfish tend to stick to a given area, for protection, for feeding or because overall conditions are at an optimum. The fish is cold, and that's another reason it won't be moving around too much. And deep ocean environments tend to be pretty stable, so scent trails will take a long time to leak out from any potential bait. We're going to have to drop the bait right on to its nose. Too far away and the fish just won't go for it.

There are still many mysteries surrounding this most elusive of fish. This is one reason why fishing them in huge numbers, given that we don't fully understand their basic ecology, let alone their breeding habits, is a hellishly bad idea.

That night in the restaurant the team apprise their waiter of the bold plan they have in mind, only to be told the attempt is 'madness'. But Charlie and the team are made of stern stuff. They do manage to get one tip from the waiter. His friend Fabian, he tells them, is a fisherman who just might be able to help the boys out.

Local knowledge has proved its worth over and over again, so this is an opportunity too good to pass up. Taking to a kayak, Jay and Charlie paddle across a steel-grey lake to meet the savant.

Meanwhile Blowfish has been exploring the seashore. He's found thousands of mussels – and that's an encouraging sign for the fishing ahead.

BLOWFISH:

'YOU GET COLD WATER IN AREAS WHERE YOU GET A LOT OF WAVES AND WINDS. AND THAT MOVEMENT STIRS UP NUTRIENTS. THE WATERS ROUND HERE ARE SO RICH – THEY'RE ABSOLUTELY FULL OF PLANKTON. AND PLANKTON MEANS PRODUCTIVITY, IT'S THE START OF A MASSIVE FOOD CHAIN THAT MANY ANIMALS LOOK TO EXPLOIT. THE SOUTHERN OCEAN IS ONE OF THE RICHEST IN THE WORLD.'

Blowfish also spots a fish trap on the beach – and that gives him an idea. And Jay has also had a revelation, watching Fabian winding up his line on to a cylinder turned by a handle.

JAY:

'I'M WORRIED THAT BECAUSE THE TOOTHFISH ARE SO FAR DOWN, IF WE DO HAPPEN TO HOOK ONE, THERE ARE GOING TO BE PREDATORS AFTER THAT TOOTHFISH AS WE'RE REELING IT UP. SPERM WHALES, SEA LIONS. SO WHATEVER YOU DO, YOU'VE GOT TO RETRIEVE THAT FISH FAST.'

Fabian, it turns out, when he considers the boys' request to take them fishing for toothfish, is cut from the same pessimistic cloth as his waiter friend. He tells them that not only can he not take them out in his boat – it's far too small given the restless nature of the South Atlantic seas – but, for the same reason, they have absolutely no chance whatsoever of catching toothfish with a rod. Apart from that … it's a great plan.

But Fabian does offer a crumb of comfort. To have any possibility of success, he tells them, they have to go to Ushuaia – on the very tip of Tierra del Fuego – to charter a much larger boat than his: at least 40 metres long, compared to his 7.

There's no choice – the team just has to go to Ushuaia, or abandon hope. Pronounced 'Ooswyah', Ushuaia likes to bill itself as the most southerly city on the planet, the edge of the inhabited world. It's home to nearly 60,000 people, and it's a thriving resort as well as a fishing port, boasting the world's southernmost ski resort and golf course. But its main attraction for tourists is as a stopping-off point before crossing over to the 'seventh continent', Antarctica.

There's more disturbing news when Charlie, Blowfish and Jay go down to the harbour to ask advice of the professionals. You need a boat like that, one of the fisherman tells them, pointing over to a tanker-like floating slab that's as big, Blowfish remarks, as a small village. And that's not all. The commercial fishermen, it turns out, don't catch toothfish anywhere near Ushuaia. You have to go to the deep South Pacific off the coast of Chile, they're told. Or even Australia. Or the Malvinas. The usual crushing sweetener is added: 'I wish you all the luck in the world.'

With that ambiguous encouragement ringing in their ears, the boys contemplate the complete failure of their mission. With just four days to go, the toothfish has made itself even more elusive than ever.

CHARLIE:
'MY DREAM OF US BECOMING THE FIRST RECREATIONAL FISHERMEN TO CATCH THE DELICIOUS TOOTHFISH IS IN TATTERS. NOT ONLY DO WE NEED A COMMERCIAL TRAWLER, WE'RE ALSO IN COMPLETELY THE WRONG COUNTRY. I TOTALLY UNDERESTIMATED THIS MISSION.'

But *'the Malvinas'* suddenly rings a bell – it's the archipelago known in Britain as the Falkland Islands. The scene of a war between Britain and Argentina in 1982, and still disputed territory. And a topic that visiting British television crews are best advised to treat with caution.

That night, Charlie makes a desperate series of mercy calls and finally the boys are invited to come and fish in the Falklands. The next day they take

a small plane and fly the 800 kilometres from Ushuaia to the capital, Port Stanley. The islands, when they come into view, look utterly desolate. But as they draw nearer the scenery starts to remind Charlie of Dartmoor, with its mossy, rocky tors, rivers and estuaries, and beautiful birds of prey. For Jay, whose regiment served in the Falklands War and fought at Goose Green, it's a weird experience to be coming here to fish.

Just over 2,500 people live on the islands; but between them they catch over 200,000 tonnes of fish each year, including toothfish. And what's more, Charlie tells Blowfish and Jay, here there's some of the best sea trout fishing in the world. That's first on the agenda. Especially when it turns out to be a beautiful sunny day, with blue skies to match the blue seas.

When they get to the fishing spot recommended by their hosts, a stretch of estuary between two islands, the boys see big sea trout rising straight away, as the nutrient-rich water is teeming with them. But Blowfish, who's still a reluctant novice with rod and line, is despondent about his chances. Until, that is, he catches a magnificent trout, well over a kilogram, much to his surprise. Jay, also using a spinner, follows suit – and so does Charlie, with a shrimp fly. All in all, a much-needed confidence boost: the toothfish now await.

FACT FILE **THE FALKLAND ISLANDS**

The Falkland Islands are situated on the 'Patagonian Shelf' and near the 'Antarctic Convergence', where the Antarctic waters meet those of the slightly warmer sub-Antarctic. The location makes for rich marine life and rich fishing.

The Falklands comprise the larger islands of West and East Falkland, and 776 smaller islets. The islands take their name from Falkland Sound, which was christened by a British naval captain in 1690. Europeans are thought to have made landfall a century or more earlier. We do know that the islands changed hands with bewildering rapidity thereafter, being settled in turn by the French, the Spanish and the Argentinians, while the British, as was their wont, claimed them for the British Crown in 1765.

The Falklands War of 1982 baffled many observers, since the islands hadn't been of strategic importance since the days of the tall ships. The economy is based on sheep-farming and fishing, hardly a unique prize. The great Argentinian writer Jorge Luis Borges described the conflict as 'two bald men fighting over a comb'. But in the 1970s it had been suggested that there was oil off the Falklands. Black gold. It turns out that there may be up to a billion barrels of the stuff, deep under the sea, within 200 nautical miles of the islands – the largest cache of hydrocarbons in British territory outside the North Sea.

Charlie has borrowed the 70-metre *Protegat*. In its day job it's a fishery patrol vessel – it's now been recruited to serve in Operation Toothfish. The voyage, under the command of another Charlie, a Scot, soon gets under way, with the red ensign fluttering in the breeze. This huge vessel will be the boys' home for the next two days. Overnight, they'll be sailing 160 kilometres to the best deep-sea fishing ground. Their mission will start at first light.

Once the team wake up out in the South Atlantic, there's no time to waste: the baited hooks need to be launched into the sea as soon as possible, to give them maximum opportunity to work their magic. Charlie has accepted that a rod and line just won't work here. The seabed is more than a kilometre down. 'Longlining' is the only answer. But on a very, very modest scale.

'I WANT US TO BE THE FIRST RECREATIONAL FISHERMEN TO CATCH A TOOTHFISH.
THAT MEANS AROUND A DOZEN HOOKS AND NO FANCY MACHINERY, JUST LOTS OF
BAIT AND SOME HELP FROM JAY AND BLOWFISH TO REEL THE LINE IN.'

FACT FILE TOOTHFISH AND OVER-FISHING

Fishing for toothfish only really got going in the 1970s. Mostly, they were caught accidentally, as the 'bycatch' of trawlers fishing close to the seabed. The shortage of cod, come the 1980s – thanks to over-fishing – saw the commercial fishing of toothfish go into overdrive. Longlining took over from trawling. The lines live up to their name and can reach a depth of 2 kilometres or more. Up to a staggering 10,000 hooks are used. With grim predictability, toothfish, by the next decade, were declining in numbers too. Legislation was passed to try to reduce the catch, but 'IUU' – illegal, unregulated and unreported fishing – made things even worse. Thankfully, in the last decade or so, much of this illegal fishing has been curtailed – although, by repute, some still goes on.

Longlining has considerable drawbacks. It can damage the seabed, and it creates bycatch, not just of other, untargeted (and illegal to fish) marine species, but also of seabirds. This includes the magnificent albatross – the bird species with the greatest wingspan of any, and sadly, one that's under severe threat, longlining being the main cause. The birds try to take the bait off the hooks, get tangled in the lines, and drown.

But this has been slowly changing: all fishing boats are now legally required to take precautions to try to ensure that bycatch does not occur. The dumping of waste – including plastics – has been outlawed. Fishing is forbidden in territorial waters, in waters shallower than 500 metres and in protected areas. In order to minimize the danger to seabirds, weights are attached to the lines to make them sink faster, and flapping streamers are tied on to scare off the birds. Setting hooks is done at night, when they can't be seen. Reports suggest that seabird mortalities in the Falkland Islands as a result of longline fishery have been zero since 2007. If so, this is a very encouraging sign.

Charlie and Jay skewer a rank mixture of squid and sardine on to the dozen hooks, and securely tie the weights so the line sinks straight to the bottom. Jay spots some albatrosses nearby, clearly attracted by all the frantic activity, but too late to be tempted by the baited line. This is surely a sign of good luck, as Jay tells the others.

Having launched the line 1,000 metres down into the deep, the question now arises: how are they going to get it up again? Jay unveils his clever wheeze. Yesterday, he commissioned a Falklands handyman to make him his own patent longline reeling device, and, unbeknown to Blowfish and Charlie, he's had it smuggled aboard. All is now revealed. The back wheel of a bike has been taken off and replaced with two flat discs the size of large pizzas, with a groove in the middle. By furiously cycling on this toothfish-wrangling exercise bike the boys can bring up the line far more quickly than by hand. And, ideally, quick enough so that any toothfish that may have been caught won't have been eaten by third parties.

After several hours, the boys decide to haul up whatever they've hooked. It's time for Charlie to start pedalling. And keep pedalling – the line is heavy, and it is hard work. But the auguries are good: Jay and Charlie are sure that something is on the line.

CHARLIE:

'I'M CONVINCED WE'VE CAUGHT A TOOTHFISH. WE'VE BEEN PEDALLING FOR TWENTY MINUTES, I JUST CAN'T STOP THINKING ABOUT THE WHITE GOLD THAT COULD BE ON THE OTHER END.'

Then calamity. The line suddenly snaps on the improvised bicycle reel. It looks like the line just wasn't strong enough – the fish, remember, might weigh up to about 100 kilos.

Only one thing for it: they need a stronger line. And the only one available is the one Blowfish has brought with him – he's been pursuing his own contribution to Operation Toothfish. Taking his cue from the fish trap he saw out in Tierra del Fuego, he's commissioned his own bespoke, environmentally friendly toothfish trap, made by an island craftsman out of recycled material.

And now there's a South American stand-off. Blowfish is absolutely convinced that his trap is the way to go. Charlie is absolutely convinced that the longline is their only hope. Jay tries to act as honest broker, but … it's Charlie's challenge; Blowfish graciously gives in, though with a heavy heart. His rope is put at the disposal of the longlining scheme. It's quickly baited and hurled over the side. Down it quickly sinks and that's it for another six hours.

Then it's back on the bike to reel the line back in. It was tough before; now with the heavier line it's backbreaking work. With, it turns out, no reward. Although something has definitely been nibbling the bait, there are no fish on the hooks whatsoever. That's not a surprise – up to half the toothfish captured on commercial longlines, it's reckoned, fall prey to passing whales, seals and occasionally squid as they're reeled in. Speed is of the essence – little wonder the professionals use heavy-duty mechanized winches. But this is sports fishing – that kind of thing would be against the code.

And so it's got to be third time lucky. Blowfish again puts forward the merits of his trap – but Charlie has got the bit between his teeth. The longline rules. The next morning, though, the three of them have to go back to Port Stanley. This is it, now or never. The line is re-baited and put back into the water so as to work its – admittedly, waning – magic for ten hours overnight. The next morning, the boys are very nervous indeed about what results await them. Frantically, they start pedalling. Jay, ever the optimist, is again convinced that something is on the line. But, sadly, his confidence is again misplaced: nothing is on the line, except for a sorry collection of bare hooks. Crabs and small fish, Blowfish sadly concludes, have just had a free buffet.

CHARLIE:

'WE'VE KNOWN ALL ALONG IT WAS GOING TO BE TOUGH AND IT'S ONLY NOW, I SUPPOSE, THAT WE'VE REALIZED HOW TOUGH IT ACTUALLY WAS. BUT THAT'S WHY WE DID IT. YOU COULD CHOOSE TO BASE YOUR ADVENTURES ON NORMAL FISHING TECHNIQUES – BUT THAT WOULD BE BORING. WE'RE ALMOST CERTAINLY THE FIRST PEOPLE TO COME OUT AND FISH FOR TOOTHFISH WITH A PUSHBIKE: BUT IT'S BEEN AN INCREDIBLE EXPERIENCE. THE IMPOSSIBLE IS WHAT MAKES IT WORTH DOING.'

But the boys do get their hands on a toothfish after all – filleted and cooked by the captain, who has taken pity on them and laid on a toothfish supper. One he caught earlier, and almost certainly by more conventional means. Was it worth the wait? It's a bit like a buttery lobster, Charlie concludes – very fatty, very meaty, not like eating fish at all. But they can all see what the fuss is about – and it goes down a treat.

Time for a toast, and there can only be one: 'Gentlemen, the toothfish: next time.'

LAOS

THE LOCATION: LAOS

THE FISH: DEVIL CATFISH

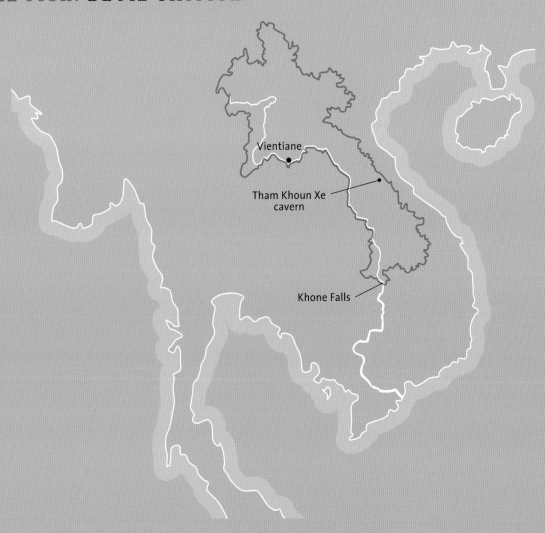

Vientiane

Tham Khoun Xe
cavern

Khone Falls

JAY, CHARLIE AND BLOWFISH have plenty of experience between them where fish and fishing are concerned. But none of them has ever been asked to catch a fish that takes them into the realms of the Underworld. Until now. Charlie's challenge here in Laos, on the mighty Mekong River, is not only for the team to find, and catch, a 'devil catfish': they are going to have to propitiate the spirit world before they embark on their search for this legendary creature.

Laos is the 'rice bowl' of Asia, and at its heart lies the Mekong River, *Mae Nam Khong*. In terms of length, at 4,350 kilometres it's the world's twelfth longest river; in terms of biodiversity it ranks second, pipped only by the Amazon. The Mekong rises in the Tibetan plateau and passes through China, Myanmar, Laos, Thailand and Cambodia before joining the South China Sea at the Mekong Delta, in Vietnam. Over 1,000 fish species have been recorded here. It's the world's largest inland fishery, accounting for around a quarter of global freshwater catch. Here, apart from the devil catfish, swim the Irrawaddy dolphin, the giant freshwater stingray and the Mekong giant catfish. Twenty years ago the Mekong was a miracle of biodiversity, but thanks to over-fishing, and the construction of hydro-electric dams, that is under threat.

With its golden temples, or 'wats', wooden villages, crumbling colonial relics (Laos was part of French Indochina until 1953), mountains, green paddy-fields, jungles, bamboo forests, river islands, caves and waterfalls, this is an impressive and beautiful country, a land of mist, and mystery. Its people are famously courteous and gentle. But there is another side to Laos that is far less pretty. It is one of the poorest countries in east Asia, especially in rural areas, where 80% of the population live. And it bears the deep scars of a violent history.

Laos has been under a communist government since 1975, the year the Vietnam War ended (the American War, as the Vietnamese call it). During that conflict Laos – used by the Vietcong as a supply route to South Vietnam, via the Ho Chi Minh Trail – achieved the unhappy distinction of being the most heavily bombed country in the history of the world. There is still an untold amount of unexploded ordnance – including particularly deadly 'cluster' bombs – covering a quarter of the country. Cold-shouldered by the West once the war ended, Laos has recently recognized the value of tourism, and this enigma of a country has begun to open its doors and share its secrets and treasures with western tourists. Not least, visiting anglers.

The creature that has drawn Charlie, Blowfish and Jay here isn't a little beast. The devil catfish can grow up to 2 metres long, and weigh around 25 kilos. It's found in rivers in the Indian subcontinent (where it's known as the 'goonch') and all over south-east Asia. There are more than 3,000 species of catfish across the world: very little is known about this one. It's not often seen, and is rarely caught. But it broke cover dramatically in the late 90s, when reports surfaced that it was responsible for fatal attacks on humans in the Kali River in India. For a while this made the devil catfish the O. J. Simpson of the riverine world, with sensational press stories about fearsome-toothed man-eating monsters. Subsequent investigations into these incidents have suggested that the goonch was the innocent victim in a case of mistaken identity.

Charlie's plan is to tempt this elusive creature with an offer it can't refuse. An olfactory one. The number one scent that signals to big fish that smaller fish are present – and thus on the menu – is that of ammonia.

AMMONIA

Ammonia is the primary waste product of all fish, excreted mainly through the gills. Predators are not just mildly attracted by the smell of ammonia; they are *driven* to follow it. Ammonia-rich waste is to fish what carbon dioxide is to us; whatever we do, it's always there and always being produced. Mosquitoes find humans by tracking CO_2; predatory fish, such as the giant catfish, find their prey by tracking ammonia. And not just live fish: when a dead fish is broken down by bacteria, the first thing we find is a spike in the ammonia levels as decomposition begins. And the catfish is supremely well equipped to follow this trail.

Catfish are swimming tongues. They have a humungous number of taste buds; their bodies are literally coated with them, all the way down to their fins – a greater concentration than in any other animal.

As you'd expect, the greatest number of taste buds is around the mouth – but especially in the barbels, the cat-like 'whiskers'. These long whiskers help the catfish to locate their prey in a muddy, murky river where visibility is low, or non-existent.

But how is Charlie proposing to outbid the ammonia that's already present in the water, thanks to the obliging exertions of live fish and the posthumous contributions of dead ones? This is the clever bit. Or at least, he hopes it is because it's the ratchet on which the whole challenge turns. Charlie has identified a secret weapon: his aim is to get hold of some of the smelliest, most ammonia-laced ground bait naturally available on the planet, and lob it into the Mekong. This done, he assures Jay and Blowfish, devil catfish will come homing in on the stuff like shoppers at the January sales.

Blowfish immediately twigs the identity of this pong-laden panacea: *guano*. That's the genteel way of putting it, of course.

FACT FILE GUANO

Guano is a Spanish word, derived from an ancient Peruvian one. The Incas for centuries harvested the extremely pungent seabird droppings on tiny islands off their coasts – it's the most potent natural fertilizer there is. Indeed, anyone messing about in these islands was put under sentence of death, so valuable was the birds' unwitting contribution to Inca agriculture. Europeans caught on to this magical mixture in the early nineteenth century, and fortunes were made in what became known as the 'guano boom'. Tonnes upon tonnes of the stuff were scraped off the islands – largely by Chinese labourers – and shipped back to Europe, where it played a crucial part in the development of modern intensive farming methods.

Charlie, Jay and Blowfish are in a landlocked country. Seabirds, and their calling cards, are going to be hard to find. So this is where another creature whose droppings are highly prized for their fertilizing properties comes into the story. Bats. Bat poo may not be quite as potent as that of seabirds; but the fact that the ancient Chinese used it to make gunpowder tells us that it's feisty enough.

This is why the team have started their challenge in the heart of the jungle, on the Xe Bang Fai River, in Khammouane province, east central Laos. This river is one of the Mekong's many tributaries and it flows through one of the biggest caves in south-east Asia, Tham Khoun Xe. The cave houses a multitudinous

variety of bats, from Geoffroy's rousette to Theobald's tomb bat, the great roundleaf bat, the diadem roundleaf bat and – though there is some scholarly dispute about this – Pratt's roundleaf bat. This is therefore the perfect place to harvest the necessary bait.

Here, then, is stage one of Charlie's mission. But it's not going to be a question of blundering straight in. The team's guide explains that the people of the village believe the cave is home not only to bats, but also to spirits. Bad spirits, that need placating. This is an obstacle not normally covered in the fishing manual.

Of course, the villagers don't ask that Blowfish, Jay and Charlie share their beliefs, but the team would hate to offend local sensibilities by dismissing them, colonial style. They need to get a blessing before entering the cave, they're told; and to do this they need to make an offering to the spirits, an edible one. To catch a fish in the river behind the guest house will surely pose no problems to the well-oiled angling machine that is *Fishing Impossible*. It had better not do – the ceremony is scheduled for that same evening.

To cover the bases the boys carefully choose their favoured weapons. Blowfish is going with a hand-line; Jay, the spear-fisherman, carves himself a harpoon fired by a rubber band; Charlie grabs his trusty rod and line. None of them catch anything at all.

The villagers – as so often, it's local knowledge that digs any fisherman out of a hole – now lend a hand. Nets are the answer here. Specifically, 'seine nets', or dragnets, weighted in the middle, the use of which dates back to the Stone Age. And this is where Blowfish, as a heavy metal marine biologist, comes into his own. The local fishermen ask if someone can help them out by making a lot of noise, to scare the fish into their nets. Blowfish leaps and crashes into the water like a demented killer whale and a handful of baffled fish are soon shooed into

FACT FILE SPIRITS

Sixty per cent of Laotians are Buddhists. Most of the rest of the population profess Satsana Phi – the 'religion of the gods'. And Buddhism is often melded with elements of this ancient folk religion, most strongly in rural areas. Each locality has its own specific set of beliefs. Satsana Phi is an 'animist' world-view. Its adherents believe that animals, plants and places have a spirit, or soul, and that these 'anima' can take a hand in human affairs. There are 'tutelary' gods protecting buildings and territories, wild spirits associated with rivers and forests, ancestral spirits, and malevolent spirits, who are often thought to be the souls of people who have died by violent or unfortunate means and haven't been reincarnated.

the net. They're minuscule, but luckily the blessing does not have a minimum entry requirement; they'll do.

And so the ceremony can go ahead. The villagers have turned up in force – no doubt curious as to who these crazed people are who want to dice with death and enter the haunted cave. The village elder officiates, the offering is presented, and the blessing is made. To round off the ritual, rice wine, the traditional tipple of south-east Asia, is drunk through foot-long straws. White strings made of cotton are tied around Charlie's, Jay's and Blowfish's wrists to symbolize the protection against evil spirits that has been conferred. These amulets are going to be needed the very next morning – it's time to enter the Bat Cave.

The entrance to the cave is a tunnel guarded by mighty boulders, a rocky and forbidding maw set into a huge cliff. It really does look like the portal of the Underworld – little wonder the local people don't like to venture in. Since the cave was first penetrated by French explorers in 1905, only a handful of people have actually been here. The system wasn't even mapped until 2008. We now know that the Xe Bang Fai River flows through the cave for over 7 kilometres. The boys are entering this heart of darkness by rubber kayak.

BLOWFISH:
'GENTLEMEN, YOUR JOURNEY INTO THE SPIRIT WORLD STARTS RIGHT NOW.
LET'S HOPE IT'S NOT A ONE-WAY TICKET.'

The cave is gargantuan: its cathedral-like vaults climb 120 metres high and stretch 200 metres wide. Even Blowfish is forced to admit that this is bigger than anything he's seen in Yorkshire. Soon the natural light gives out and the team grope their way through by torchlight. It's eerie, atmospheric, Styx-like, and deafeningly silent. No bird sounds, no wind whispers. Just the lapping of the paddles in the water.

Then Blowfish, Jay and Charlie hear the sound of crashing rapids in the distance. Disembarking to clamber over rocks in order to reach the bat colonies, they pass strange bulbous limestone sediments – Jay thinks they look like dragon eggs – that were formed by millions of years of mineral-rich water flowing over the stones and evaporating, leaving the residue behind.

After several hours of slipping and sliding over the rocks, the boys hear the sound they've been waiting for: the squeaking, screeching and chirping of bats. Soon, they only need to follow their noses: the pungent, acrid smell of bat poo leads them to their quarry. In the gloom they can now make out the dark, huddled contours of thousands of bats. Like cash-starved miners in the '49 California gold rush, they eagerly scoop up their bounty with their kayak paddles.

The first part of the mission is accomplished; the only thing left to do now is to use the guano to catch a devil catfish. But Charlie hasn't told the guys that he doesn't really have any idea how they're actually going to use the bat poo as bait.

Ammonia is highly soluble in water and disperses quickly. So once the guano becomes diluted in the river, the catfish's sense of taste – and smell – will alert it to the possibilities ahead. A well-used fishing trick when it comes to putting groundbait in the water silently and accurately is to use a catapult. Jay sets and fires, and within minutes he catches a Java barb, a beautiful fish with shining silver lozenge-shaped scales. Like the catfish, it too has an acute sense of smell. The guano seems to be working its magic on smaller fish, so the team make their final journey south to the lower reaches of the mighty Mekong, to see if they can acquaint a devil catfish with the wonder bait. They travel 500 kilometres to the southern tip of Laos, where the Cambodian border snakes around to join that of Vietnam, cutting off Laos from the sea. This region is one of the most popular with tourists – and it's easy to see why. The Khone Falls, where the team pitch up, are breathtaking, a riot of rock, water and foam.

FACT FILE **THE KHONE FALLS**

The Khone Falls are a spectacular series of cataracts that marks the division between the upper and lower navigation of the Mekong. As the river enters Cambodia, 95% of its tributaries have now joined the main flow. Every year more than 500 billion cubic metres of water is washed down into the South China Sea. The Khone Falls are the biggest in south-east Asia, the longest drop being 21 kilometres. The whole area – the country's richest fishing grounds – is known as Si Phan Don: '4,000 islands'. Monsoons drench south-west Laos from May to October, and the volume of water in the 4,000 islands is increased thirty times – the biggest seasonal change in water volume of any river in the world. The combined watercourse is 14 kilometres across at its widest point. This super-abundance plays a central role in determining the patterns of migration of 135 species of fish along the Mekong. It has done for centuries – it may not do for much longer.

Half the 4,000 islands are submerged during the wet season. The whole area is then known to the local people as the 'Flooded Forest'. Every flood-prone society in the world has its own ancient myths to explain the phenomenon. In Britain we are, perhaps, beginning to develop our own. The Laotians believe that the flooded forest hides the palace of a water serpent, Ngeuak, queen of the Underworld. The catfish swimming in these waters are said to be under her direct command. Rather worryingly, she is particularly feared because of her fondness for devouring drowning fishermen.

The team are here in December and so the monsoon waters have subsided. To get a measure of the Mekong, and to find out how the locals fish, Charlie takes the boys to one of the islands. There's no ferry across the Mekong: the island Charlie has his eye on can only be reached by shuffling yourself, *mano a mano,* along a rope slung over the terrifying and tumultuous torrents.

Having safely passed across to the other side, Jay, Blowfish and Charlie join the Laos fishermen – and fisherboys – casting nets into the roiling water. These 'throw nets' are 10 metres in diameter, and weighted at the edges. The art of casting them can take years to master, and the team have only got a few hours. Nonetheless, Blowfish gets the hang of it sufficiently to net a little goby, a fish which has come up with an ingenious wheeze so it can stick to the rocks in these turbulent waters like a toy arrow: it fuses its pelvic fins together to form a sucker. The waters here are too rapid and violent to be the favoured fishing grounds of the devil catfish.

To recce a more likely spot, Charlie takes to a kayak; and he finds what he takes to be a good fishing ground 3 kilometres away from the falls. What catfish like, he's been advised by the local guides, is a nice fast-flowing river with deep pools and a rocky or gravelly bed. Here the catfish can lie incognito until their prey swim into view.

The next phase is to 'chum' the water. And this is where the ammonia-rich bat guano is going to play a starring role. But Charlie wants to add an extra layer of insurance. Jay and Blowfish are sent to a local market to pick up the smelliest bait they can find, to add to the great guano cocktail.

BLOWFISH:
'WE'VE GOT LARGE INTESTINES, SMALL INTESTINES, WE'VE GOT KIDNEYS, WE'VE GOT LIVERS, YOU NAME AN INTERNAL ORGAN, WE'VE BAGGED IT'.

The fishing spot is primed with Charlie's pedigree chum – by means of a patent bamboo cannon – and the team wait for the bait to settle. When they start fishing, though, it's immediately apparent that this is going to be even more of a challenge than Charlie had feared. He's convinced there are big catfish hiding in the deep pools. But there are huge clumps of weed barrelling down the river, which constantly snag the lines. And the catfish, if hooked, aren't going to give up the fight easily: they will swim past submerged rocks, trees and roots and try to use them to create tension so as to snap the line. For this reason, in such terrain, anglers use a 'leader', a strong abrasive-resistant line, in this case of around six metres, that attaches to the hook. After six hours, the team have only managed to catch a fine collection of weeds. It's a sombre evening back at base.

CHARLIE:
'THIS HAS BEEN THE TOUGHEST FISHING EXPERIENCE OF MY LIFE. EVERYTHING ABOUT THIS RIVER IS HARD WORK. THE WATER IS DEEP AND FAST-FLOWING, AND THERE'S ACRES OF WEED COMING DOWN WITH THE CURRENT. IT TAKES A LOAD OF LEAD WEIGHT TO KEEP THE BAIT ON THE BOTTOM, AND SO THERE'S NOT ENOUGH SENSITIVITY TO REALLY TELL IF THERE'S A BITE OR NOT. AND THE WEED COLLECTING ON THE LINE DRAGS IT DOWNRIVER. IT'S NOT LIKE ANYTHING I HAVE FISHED IN BEFORE.

On the final day, the guano and guts having further primed the fishing spot overnight, suddenly there's better luck. Charlie hooks a red catfish. But it's a small one; they're running out of time if they want to catch the giant devil. The team now double up their armoury, setting more rods in the river, on the opposite bank, watched over by the camera crew. And it's the usually unseen warriors of *Fishing Impossible* who now get the lucky strike. It's not a devil catfish – but it's a big one, and a much rarer member of the family. So rare as far as biologists are concerned – but no doubt not the local fishers, who will have caught it before – that it hasn't even had time to acquire an English nickname since it was first classified in 2006. It goes, instead, under the magnificent monicker *Wallago micropogon*. It may be an obscure member of the family tree, but it's a beauty for all that.

CHARLIE:
'WE WERE LOOKING FOR A DEVIL CATFISH BUT CAUGHT A FISH THAT'S ACTUALLY FAR RARER. FISHING IS WEIRD LIKE THAT. MAYBE THAT'S WHY I LOVE IT SO MUCH.'

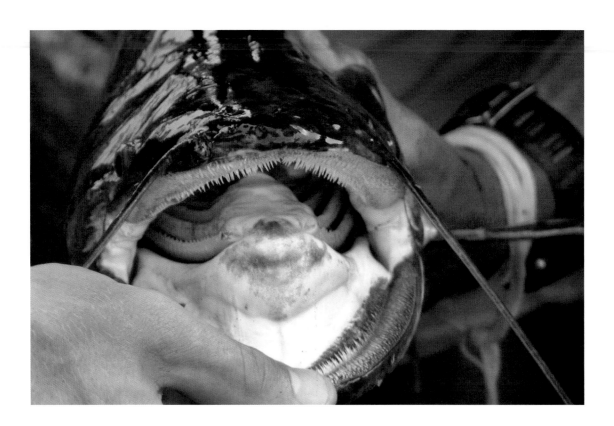

If the team basked in a warm glow after catching the *Wallago micropogon*, the bait they caught it with will be less fondly remembered. To try to make sure of that, they all threw their clothes away, so impossible was it to get rid of the stench. But what will leave an even more lasting impression, sadly, is the state of the Mekong itself.

CHARLIE:
'IT'S THE MOST BEAUTIFUL PLACE YOU COULD IMAGINE, AND FROM THE STORIES I'VE HEARD THE FISHING MUST ONCE HAVE BEEN INCREDIBLE. BUT NOW IT'S A DEAD RIVER. THERE ARE NOT MANY BIG FISH LEFT. IT'S A TRAGEDY, AND WE ALL FELT THAT.'

JAY:
'YOU HAVE TO SEE IT TO BELIEVE IT HOW MANY LINES, HOOKS AND NETS THERE WERE IN THE WATER. A RIVER LIKE THIS SHOULD BE FILLED WITH FISH. BUT IT'S BEEN DESTROYED.'

BLOWFISH:
'IT'S HEARTBREAKING, THERE'S NO OTHER WAY TO DESCRIBE IT. THE MEKONG HAS BEEN SYSTEMATICALLY HARVESTED TO THE LAST GUPPY. IN THE 70S IT WAS A BOX OF TREASURES – NOW IT'S BEEN PLUNDERED.'

FACT FILE THE MEKONG MALAISE

That the Mekong is but a shadow of its former self it is hard to deny. Local people certainly don't deny it. They are better aware than anyone that there are today fewer fish, and smaller fish, than there used to be. This is a desperately acute problem, not just for the fish or for wildlife lobbies, but for the Laotians themselves. Perhaps 50 million people rely on the Mekong for their food and for their livelihoods: this precipitous decline in fish stocks is a disaster from every conceivable point of view.

And what is extraordinary is that most of the damage has been perpetrated in just the last two decades. The Mekong giant catfish, another iconic species, has declined by 90%. Not only has there been a vast increase in subsistence fishing – more than the river can sustain – there has also been an explosion in the most brutal and damaging methods of catching fish imaginable. Dynamite, car batteries, poison, even rifles – all are, illegally, used. Micro-meshed mosquito nets, which catch juvenile fish as well as adults, have added to the disaster.

And all this, many (if not indeed, most) observers believe, is only going to get worse. There are seven dams on the upper Mekong in China, which contributes 45% of the lower Mekong's water in the dry season, with another twenty-one dams rumoured to be on the way. Eleven more (and counting) are planned in Laos and Cambodia. The government of Laos is the main mover here, aiming to boost its electricity-generating capacity by 25%, and sell some of this surplus to its neighbours. Despite its promise that the dams will have 'fish-friendly' structures that allow fish to migrate freely through them, no one believes this will work. As Blowfish puts it, 'They are just great hulking slabs of concrete slammed across the water.'

'Flood pulses' in the river provide the signal for the fish to migrate; obviously they need sufficient water in which to do so. The finished dams are already interfering with both of these processes. And the major fish migrations provide up to 70% of the commercial fishing catch in the Mekong. Even the official inter-governmental body of Laos, Cambodia and Vietnam, the 'Mekong River Commission', estimated in 2010 that the proposed dams could cause the loss of between 26% and 42% of fish, and lead to the displacement of 100,000 people. It recommended a ten-year moratorium before any more dams were built. The Laos government has set aside this advice, and is pressing on. Unless this programme is halted, in a few years' time fishing for giant catfish here in the Mekong will be quite literally *Fishing Impossible.*

SOUTH AFRICA

THE LOCATION: SOUTH AFRICA

THE FISH: GREAT WHITE SHARK

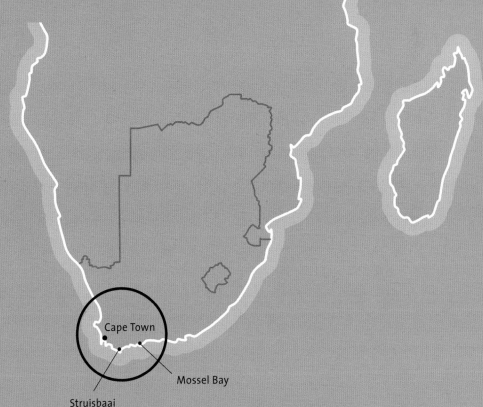

Cape Town

Mossel Bay

Struisbaai

THE GREAT WHITE SHARK.

If the very name doesn't strike terror into your heart you've probably never shared the water with one of them. Or seen a fin coming towards you. Or seen *Jaws*. Or perhaps you're a marine biologist.

Blowfish: 'When I was about seven or eight, I was tricked by my next-door neighbour into watching a very famous film, with a very famous soundtrack, and it scared the hell out of me. I wouldn't have my feet over the edge of the bed, didn't want to go in the sea, wouldn't swim in a swimming pool on my own. Then I went through the Shark Tunnel at a very famous prison called Seaworld in Florida and came out the other side, just buzzing, absolutely buzzing. I said to my mum, I want to be a marine biologist.'

Reasoning that learning about sharks would allay his fears, Blowfish has spent his life studying them. But to learn about sharks is not only to learn about their characteristics, and the vital role they play in marine ecology; it's also to realize the scale of the threat they are under from their only real predator, apart from the killer whale. Guess who.

In recent decades marine biologists have made great strides in discovering the secrets of sharks. Sophisticated GPS tags now tell us about population numbers, and, fascinatingly, where sharks actually go. (It's only been realized in the last two decades or so that the great white shark migrates huge distances and swims to incredible depths – why, we're still not really sure.) And yet we've never seen a great white give birth. We still have plenty to learn.

Tagging sharks in order to learn about them is problematic. The larger ones have to be caught and hauled out of the water. They can survive this if it's done efficiently and quickly, but inevitably some trauma to the shark is involved. And this, naturally, doesn't sit well with a body of people whose aim is to study and protect the shark, not cause it pain or discomfort.

Blowfish's challenge to the team, then, is to find a way to tag the big sharks without resorting to bait, hook, line, sinker or net. If that sounds like a riddle – he has a solution in mind.

Charlie, Jay and Blowfish start their South African adventure with a spectacular, vertiginous cable-car ride up to the top of Table Mountain in Cape Town, South Africa's highest point.

The southern South African coast, which they can see spread out before them, looking magnificent, has the largest concentration of sharks anywhere in the world. In effect three oceans meet here. The cold, stormy Atlantic Ocean churns things up and gets them moving. The Indian Ocean is warm, and contains a rich diversity of marine life. The Southern Ocean sends an abundance of nutrients up to the Cape. Thus the three best things you could have as an environment for sea creatures are all here on South Africa's doorstep.

FACT FILE THE WESTERN CAPE

In recent decades the Western Cape has become a hot ticket among the world's major tourist destinations. There are restaurants, bars, and fabulous beaches, of course. Plus sailing, fishing, surfing, windsurfing, paragliding, sky-diving and rock climbing.

But what's truly breathtaking about the Western Cape is the sheer beauty of the flora and fauna – and this is an area of the richest biodiversity. The province is home to several national parks, wildernesses, nature reserves, mountain catchment areas and botanical gardens. The Cape Floral Region is one of only six 'floral kingdoms' in the world, a World Heritage site. The whole coast is fringed with the intense, kaleidoscopic multi-colours of fynbos ('fine bush'), the tiny flowers of the scrub and heathland. There are nearly 9,000 separate species of fynbos in the Cape; 2,000 on Table Mountain alone.

Cape Point, the rocky headland to the south of the city (the site of the famous Cape of Good Hope, so named because for a ship travelling down the coast of Africa, here the currents turn eastwards) is part of Table Mountain National Park, and home to Cape mountain zebra, chacma baboons (also endemic to the region), and antelope (klipspringer, steenbok and eland), as well as the enigmatic Cape clawless otters. Since 1982, Boulder Beach has been colonized by the rare African penguin.

The whole shore eastwards from the Cape is renowned as a site for whale-watching: the south-west strip, from Rooiels to Quoin Point, is known as the Whale Coast. Here can be seen southern right whales, humpback whales, bottlenose and common dolphins, and, occasionally, killer whales. There is also a rich diversity of smaller sea life and a multitude of bird species.

The most famous tourist destination in the Western Cape is the Garden Route, which stretches from Mossel Bay to Storms River. A strip of coast 300 kilometres long, celebrated for its spectacular views, forests, rocky shores, white sandy beaches and lagoons, the seductive names of some of the places en route – Wilderness, Garden of Eden, Nature's Valley – give a clue as to its appeal.

Inland above the Garden Route, the Karoo National Park is home to lions, rhino, buffalo, zebra, brown hyena and Verreaux's eagles, while Oudtshoorn is said to be the ostrich capital of the world.

'THESE THREE SEAS COME TOGETHER AT THE CAPE, CREATING A MARINE MOSHPIT OF AWESOMENESS. USUALLY THESE CONDITIONS, ATTRACTING SO MUCH DIVERSE SEA LIFE, HAPPEN WAY, WAY OFFSHORE. HERE IT HAPPENS BANG ON THE COAST. SO YOU SEE MASSIVE FISH: TUNA AND BILLFISH, ALONGSIDE THE OCEAN'S MAIN PREDATOR – SHARKS. AND WE'RE HERE TO BE THEIR PREDATORS. WE'RE GOING TO FISH FOR SHARKS.'

To prove it, Blowfish takes Charlie and Jay down to the beach at Struisbaai, on the southern tip of South Africa. Around 300 species of shark can be found off the coast here. This is a shark convention.

Here, champion sports fisherman Brian MacFarlane shows Jay and Charlie how to cast their lines out beyond the sandbanks into the rolling waves, where the biggest sharks are waiting. As long as the waterline stays below their chests, they are safe from danger. But as the buffeting Charlie receives from the racing current submerges him, he makes a quick retreat to shore.

While the other boys are dicing with death, Blowfish is further along the beach, where he's hooked up with some fellow marine biologists, led by Meaghen McCord, founder of the South Africa Shark Conservancy. And if this seems like chalk and cheese – fishermen at one end of the beach trying to catch sharks, and scientists down the other trying to protect them – actually the two tribes have joined forces in recent years, in what Blowfish calls 'the ultimate marriage of fishing and science'. The scientists need the fish to be caught to attach the all-important tags; the fishermen are paid to catch the fish. It's now illegal to catch certain sharks – including the great white – without a permit, and the numbers are strictly limited. Exceptions are made for licensed marine biologists involved in tagging and conservation.

FACT FILE TAGGING

A variety of tags are used to keep tabs on fish, ranging from the basic dart, or 'spaghetti' tag, up to the far more sophisticated, and far more expensive, ones such as the 'archival' tag, which stores data on a computer chip and can track large fish over long distances. A halfway house is an 'acoustic' tag, useful only for fish that don't stray too far from the shore. Acoustic tags are surgically implanted into the fish, and can be used to work out how far a fish has travelled, and at what average speed. All this information can help scientists identify population hotspots which can then – in an ideal world – be protected from over-fishing.

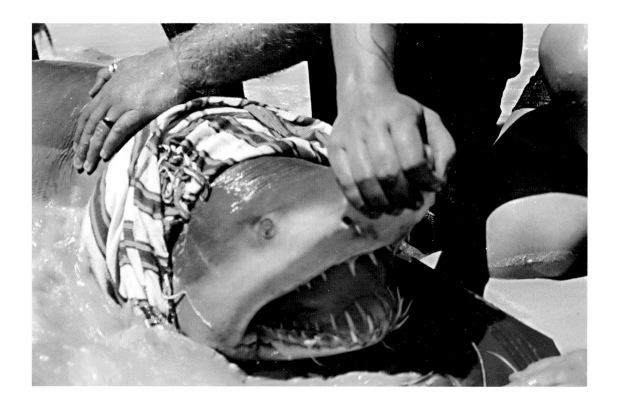

On the beach Meaghen and her team are tagging a bronze whaler shark, which, thankfully, is not fully grown. Bronze whalers are one of the shark species that can cause fatal injuries to man. Ten minutes is about the longest time a bronze whaler can survive out of water without suffering injury, so the team must work quickly. In just eight minutes the fish has been tagged and released. Blowfish has been given the job of injecting it with antibiotics, to counter any ill-effects it has suffered while out of the water. Great care also has to be taken while reeling a shark onto the beach: not having a rib cage means its internal organs can be damaged in the process.

Working back on the shore, away from danger, Charlie and Jay help the marine biologists to catch the sharks to be tagged. With considerable effort Charlie reels in a ragged tooth shark, which, at nearly 2 metres, is one of the biggest fish he's caught. It's landed next to Meaghen and her team to be tagged and released. Luckily, the ragged tooth shark is far more docile than its name might suggest. Like so many other species, it has been over-fished, not least to serve the aquarium trade. And so it's doubly important to keep tabs on its whereabouts and numbers.

Jay now hooks a fish of his own, and from the fight it puts up it's clearly a big one. Harnessing the power of the waves, he brings it in on the next rolling breaker. When it's delivered to the beach laboratory it proves to be another ragged tooth, this time a big breeding female, a shade under 2.5 metres. (A fully-grown great white shark is likely to be more than double this size.) It too is quickly tagged and released back into the water.

Tagging sharks, or any other kind of fish, is of course done in a good cause; but it would be a very welcome development if a way could be found to cause them no discomfort at all. This is what lies behind Blowfish's challenge: to find a method that allows scientists to tag fish without bringing them out of the water in the first place, and using old-fashioned fishing techniques to do so.

Charlie is sceptical: 'Catching a shark with no bait, no hooks, no lines? Blowfish has lost his mind.' Then, a fisherman Charlie meets on a research trip to a Cape Town market comes up with one way it could be done. 'If you were going to attract a shark without using bait, how would you do it?'

The answer is simple: 'Jump in the water.'

Being in the water when sharks are around is to live dangerously, if not for long. They haven't gained their fearsome reputation for nothing: one of the back-stories in *Jaws* alludes to an infamous incident in 1945, when for several days oceanic whitetip sharks repeatedly attacked and killed shipwrecked sailors who had survived the torpedoing of the USS *Indianapolis*, which was on its way back from delivering parts of the atomic bomb that destroyed Hiroshima. The sharks were attracted by the noise of the explosion and the sinking of the ship, the blood, and the survivors thrashing about in the water.

Because their attacks on humans are so spectacular, so terrifying and such good newspaper copy, we've come to regard the large sharks, and the great white in particular, one of the biggest of them all, as bundles of waterborne malevolence, cold-blooded assassins, man-eating monsters. However, this is far from accurate: there are in fact only a handful of fatalities caused by sharks each year; we have more chance of being struck by lightning.

SHARKS AND POPULATION CONTROL

Sharks play a critical role in the health of the world's oceans. As top predators, they're able to control the population numbers as well as the overall health of the different species – which they do by preying on the sick and weak. Sharks are the law enforcers of this blue planet, acting as judge, jury and executioner. Without them, chaos would reign and the seas would suffer. Studies have shown that where sharks exist in plentiful numbers and are connected within an eco-system, there is a greater diversity of species, and the species are in better health.

THE
BLOWFISH
FILE

Less than thirty of around 400 species of shark have been involved in attacks on humans; only around a dozen in fatal attacks. The great white is at the top of this league table: it's responsible for four times more human fatalities than the next one down, the tiger shark.

The shark, which has been around on the planet for 450 million years, is certainly a finely-honed killing machine, if by 'killing' we really mean 'feeding'. It's built for speed – up to 35mph at its maximum velocity. Sharks have very good eyesight, as well as an excellent sense of smell – some species can sniff out blood to the tune of one part in a million. The great white has a bite of around fifty teeth, with several rows waiting to replace those if they are lost or damaged.

Like underwater surveyors, sharks can use triangulation to locate their prey. Thanks to the marvellously named ampullae of Lorenzini (discovered in 1678 by a Florentine ichthyologist), which are electro-receptors – especially noticeable in the hammerhead – sharks can detect electric fields, including those created by swimmers and divers, long distances away. So trying to play hide and seek isn't going to work. And while no one can hear you scream in space, a shark can hear you in the water; they have extremely good hearing.

FACT FILE **SHARKS UNDER THREAT**

The total number of shark attacks on humans each year is around ten: we kill around 100 million of them per year for shark fin soup alone. The fins are sliced off and the rest of the carcase is thrown back into the water, dead or alive. Shark cadavers are also used in the making of lubricants, sandpaper and leather. They are prized in 'trophy fishing' and by the aquarium trade.

Elsewhere the assaults come thick and fast. 'Bycatch', whereby sharks (and other animals) are inadvertently taken by long lines and trawler nets along with the intended catch. 'Shark nets', put in place to protect beaches, that decimate the shark population. Add pollution and rising sea temperatures, and it's easy to see why shark populations in some areas have decreased by around 70% in just the last two or three decades. (And by as much as 90% in the Atlantic.)

And, ironically, while shark populations are going down, the number of shark attacks may actually be rising, as human populations grow, leisure time increases and more people than ever before are in the water. This is spinning out a vicious spiral that the sharks will suffer from more than us, as more attempts to protect bathers and divers are likely to reduce shark numbers further.

But, despite popular mythology, big sharks don't like to feed on us. Despite our best efforts to create an obesity crisis, humans are not fatty enough for their tastes – or rather, for their energy requirements. Many, if not most, shark attacks come about because of confusion, or curiosity. Especially if we are splashing about, or too near a potential source of food. The shark may take a bite out of a human in the water just to see if it's worth eating the whole thing. It isn't, and the sharks don't. The downside for us is that by the time the shark has turned its nose up at what we have to offer, we will very likely have bled to death.

Jay and Charlie get a sideways insight of their own into the reality of shark depopulation while they're out fishing for snoek, a kind of snake mackerel, and one of the most popular foods along the South African coast. It's the usual partner in fish and chips. But Jay and Charlie, it turns out, are not the only interested parties when it comes to catching them.

CHARLIE:
'HE'S EATING MY SNOEK!'

They're longlining and the problem is that the local seals, as soon as a fish has been hooked, swim by and help themselves, again and again. This brazen opportunist pilfering doesn't endear the seals to the local fishermen. But, as Blowfish points out, the seals' propensity for making off with someone else's dinner is not entirely their fault. The problem is that the sharks, which are the seals' natural predators, have been reduced in number here, as have the smaller fish that should make up the seals' prey. Little wonder, if their own food stocks are in short supply, that they are tempted to get stuck into fish caught by someone else.

Blowfish, while Jay and Charlie try to reel in the snoek faster than the seals can eat them, has come to a place very much after his own heart: he's paying a visit to Meaghen McCord at her very own 'Shark Laboratory'.

In order to attract sharks, so they can be caught by rod and line, or to attract small ones so they can be caught by hand, 'chumming' is often needed – a catch-all term for preparing the fishing spot with bait, either ground up (hence 'groundbait') or in the form of fish, or parts thereof. (Live bait is often used; but this is increasingly frowned upon, and not a method adopted in *Fishing Impossible*.)

Blowfish takes a diving trip with Meaghen, and manages to catch a little striped catshark (also known as a pyjama shark), using just his bare hands. This method means the shark isn't harmed, compared to reeling it in on a hook, but it wouldn't end too well for marine biologists if they tried to do this with a great white. So, along with other scientists, Meaghen has been experimenting with attracting them with a different lure, noise. In a marine biology version of *Blue Peter*, she produces a pyjama shark she prepared earlier. The small fish is placed in a large tank, into which is inserted a tube. Meaghen invites Blowfish to bang on

CHUM

Chumming is effective, but it's problematic. By luring sharks to an area using a stinky scent trail, you're essentially ringing the dinner bell. The sharks follow the chum with the idea that, at the end of the trail, there is a potential food source. So before you've even seen the shark, you can be sure it's there because it wants a feed.

Now, sharks are intelligent, and they will inspect the area for some time in search of prey before leaving to go and look elsewhere if they don't find it. The problem occurs when you attract that one shark who is desperate for food and may become a lot more unpredictable because of it. After all, we all get a bit antsy when we're hungry.

There's also a concern that chumming may lead sharks to associate human activity in the water with food. This could result in some very dangerous situations – which is why we as scientists need to think of a better way to attract them.

the tube – and the shark comes swimming over as fast as it can. Why? Because it has been trained to associate the sounds of the tube with food. This works on exactly the same principle as Pavlov's famous experiment with his dog more than a century ago.

Understandably Jay and Charlie are still somewhat sceptical about this whole proposition. But this is Blowfish's bag and so they decide to help. Their idea is to make a seal decoy to lure in the sharks, fashioned from some plywood they've found in a local hardware store. Dragging it along behind the boat, they reason, will do the trick. Blowfish, however, has something even stranger to add to the mix – at a meeting he's called at a local bar, all is revealed when Charlie and Jay walk in. Blowfish, let us remember, is a *heavy metal* marine biologist. He's sitting in on bass with a local band. Now, it's probably true to say that not many musicians would be pleased to be described as sounding like the death throes of an expiring fish. But this, it turns out, is the whole idea.

LOW FREQUENCIES

When a fish is distressed, or dying, it beats its tail. It's easy to record these tail-beats, and when they're played back to sharks they respond, thinking there is food to be had. And so if we can attract sharks by replicating these tail-beats it could mean that we can tag them without the need for old-school chumming and fishing techniques.

When an injured or dying fish squirms, it's giving off high frequencies as well as low, but the high ones are lost very quickly in the background 'noise' of waves and water. It's the low frequencies that disperse. And so heavy metal, which has rapid low frequency sounds (especially those produced by the bass), works very well as a tail-thrashing substitute.

And, interestingly, there are some frequencies which actually repel sharks. Most likely they mimic the tail-beat of a larger shark, or cetacean – either way, they think it's a predator to be avoided. This could spell good news. If we can find a suitable way of repelling sharks we can steer them away from fishing nets and public beaches.

It's fair to say that music and marine creatures have, up to now at least, rarely gone together. The nearest sharks have come to popular music is as one of the rival gangs in *West Side Story*. And those guys spent more time clicking their fingers and dancing than they did at the rumble, so they weren't really all that frightening.

Scientists have known for several decades that fish are attracted by low frequencies: what they hadn't considered was that underwater music could provide them. The idea first surfaced in Guadalupe Island, off the west coast of Mexico, when shark tour operators decided to relieve the boredom of waiting in a cage while no sharks were to be seen by playing music for their punters through underwater speakers. To their astonishment, sharks seemed to be attracted to the sound. The idea was taken up by a tour operator in South Australia, who went a step further and decided to play his customers the greatest hits of the local wild colonial boys, AC/DC . Two tracks in particular, 'You Shook Me All Night Long' and 'Back in Black', proved to be an instant hit with the shark population, which soon began to draw nearer.

Because the sharks 'bumped' the loudspeakers, usually in shark behaviour a preliminary exploration to see if something is worth taking a bite out of, it seems clear that classic Ozzie rock was able to mimic the tail-beats of a dying fish. Giving 'soundbite' a whole new meaning.

To replicate this hard rock café in South African waters, Blowfish, Charlie and Jay have come to Mossel Bay, 400 kilometres east of Cape Town. If the coast of South Africa in general is shark country, Mossel Bay is Shark City, the epicentre, the omphalos, the Times Square or Piccadilly Circus. A quorum of 'man-eaters' are here. Bronze whalers, hammerheads, and the great white itself.

The boys are in the company of Dr Enrico Gennari, a scientist and shark expert – he and his Oceans Research team are based here in the bay. An expert in tagging, Enrico is on hand to fire a harmless acoustic tag into the dorsal fin of any large shark that comes up to the speaker, using a modified spear-gun. Getting Enrico and the science bods on board doesn't prove to be too difficult – it's their boat, after all. The band is a different matter. Roadies aren't used to

setting up in a small boat. But professional pride dictates they have to give it their best shot.

Blowfish counts them in, and the music begins to play through underwater speakers, spreading the low frequency beats through the water. Will this be the magic formula to persuade the sharks that lunch is served? Not immediately, as it turns out. As is always the case with *Fishing Impossible*, the catch doesn't come too soon, spoiling all the fun.

A new recording is created on board – like the first, it's played on a loop and blasted out underwater. No sharks seem to like this selection of beats and low frequency notes either. Jay and Charlie's seal is cast out into the water, where it flutters its crudely daubed eyelashes to no avail. It's time for Plan B. Reluctantly, on Blowfish's part, chum is going to have to be the next course – a seductive purée of sardine. It's not ideal: the aim ultimately is to do away with the need for it at all where tagging sharks is concerned. But at this stage of the game it's a necessary evil.

But disaster then takes a dread hand. In the annals of rock music, drummers have found themselves incapacitated for a variety of reasons, some of them strange, some of them illegal. But they rarely suffer from seasickness during a gig. On this occasion, that's precisely what has happened.

Jay sits in. Never having played drums before, he's about to make his debut in front of the biggest audience on the planet – of sharks, that is. And the Cornish magic descends. Just as the great twentieth-century French composer Olivier Messiaen cleverly mimicked birdsong in some of his music, so Jay now sets about doing the same for dying fish. No doubt impressed with his subtle and arrhythmical use of the off-beat, two bronze whalers approach the speaker. And then more and bigger fish.

The operation – and the gig – is a success. The bronze whalers are, it's true, deemed by Enrico to be too small to tag. No great whites have approached. It turns out that a whale has just died 50 kilometres away – the absolute favourite shark food – and so all great whites in the area have been otherwise engaged. As Enrico points out, shark behaviour across all the species is not that dissimilar. So if bronze whalers fall for the deception there's no reason why other, bigger sharks won't do too. The mission complete, the boys head home satisfied.

SCOTLAND

THE LOCATION: SCAPA FLOW, ORKNEY

THE FISH: LING

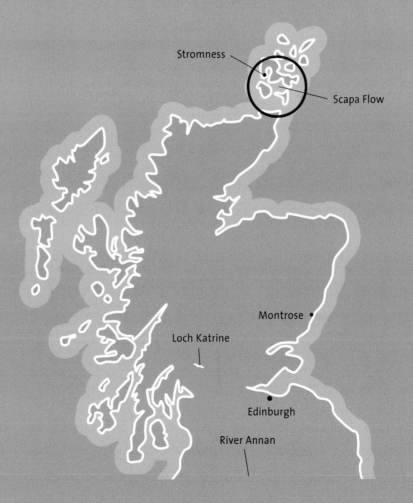

Stromness

Scapa Flow

Montrose

Loch Katrine

Edinburgh

River Annan

THE CHALLENGE

ON PAPER, JAY'S CHALLENGE SOUNDS A DODDLE.

He's taking Charlie and Blowfish to rivers, lochs and seas renowned for their excellent fishing, a magnet for thousands of visitors who come each year to do just that. The spectacular catches on offer are evidenced by dozens of websites, selfies and Instagram posts showing anglers grinning away next to the implausibly large fish they've caught. And this will be a journey through some of the most beautiful scenery in the British Isles. But there's a drawback: Jay and the boys are going to be fishing in the middle of the bleak midwinter. In the frozen north.

Jay's challenge is to fish in Scapa Flow, Orkney, for more than fifty years the most important naval base in Britain. Like many fishermen, he's dreamed of fishing here since he was a child. There are around 150 wrecks scattered on the seabed: they've become a kind of artificial cold-water reef for starfish, sea urchins, lobsters – and fish. The boys are after ling, one of the tastiest fish in British seas.

But will any fish be feeding in early January, when the water is cold and they are not too keen to race around? If not, how will Jay, Blowfish and Charlie tempt them to take any bait? This is the key to the challenge.

On their way to Orkney the team will be trying out their usual array of ingenious techniques, in some of Scotland's prime fishing locations: for brown trout in Howietoun, one of the oldest fish farms in the world; pike in Loch Katrine; grayling in the River Annan; Atlantic cod off the jagged coast of north-east Scotland. And then on to Orkney. Seventy craggy islands – of which only twenty are inhabited – fringed with towering sea cliffs, some of the highest in the British Isles. Orkney is as wild as it is magical. The scenery is austere at this time of year, but its silvery, blue-grey grandeur lends both land and water an understated raw beauty.

Winter fishing is tough, but at least the boys won't suffer from the midges that bite summer fisherpeople into a pin-cushion.

The team start their fishing tour of Scotland in some of its most beautiful waters, those of Loch Katrine, in the Trossachs. A freshwater loch, nearly 13 kilometres long, 1.5 kilometres wide and 150 metres deep at its maximum, it lies just over 2 kilometres away from the bonny banks and braes of Loch Lomond. An hour in the car from both Glasgow and Edinburgh, Loch Katrine is a popular day trip destination. The hills and forest that surround it are one of the last redoubts of the red squirrel; but it is known above all for its fishing. And it *is* fresh water: since 1859 it has served as the main water supply for the City of Glasgow, and no petrol engines are allowed on the loch.

Blowfish and Charlie begin exploring the water on the small but elegant SS *Sir Walter Scott*, which has been sailing here since 1900. The steamship now runs on biofuel. Its choice of name gives us a clue as to the distinguished literary past of Loch Katrine: it played a starring role in the development of British Romanticism.

Loch Katrine is best known for its brown trout – but in January they're in close season. The main catch at this time of year is the loch's apex predator – the fearsomely aggressive, razor-toothed and powerful pike. The pike in Loch Katrine were only introduced around the time Sir Walter Scott was writing about the area.

FACT FILE LOCH KATRINE AND THE ROMANTICS

Glengyle, on Loch Katrine, was the birthplace of one of Scotland's greatest heroes, Rob Roy MacGregor. The name Katrine means cattle thief. How many head of cattle a clan chief owned was a mark of his eminence, and if he didn't feel he had enough he was quite happy to make up the numbers by taking them from a rival clan. Rob Roy was such a cattle stealer – this was airbrushed somewhat in his later legend so as to make him into a Scottish Robin Hood. He fought in the first Jacobite war of 1689, in support of the deposed Catholic James II (James VII of Scotland), and took part in the Rising of 1715, ending up with a price on his head.

A century after this, Sir Walter Scott, the most famous and widely read author of his day, a pillar of the Romantic movement, put him into print with his novel *Rob Roy*. He did the same for Loch Katrine itself, which he used as the setting for his immensely successful long poem, *The Lady of the Lake*, published in 1810 (and turned into an opera, *La donna del lago*, by Rossini).

Wordsworth had also been to Loch Katrine, in 1803, and he too composed poems inspired by the beauty of the region – and its young female inhabitants. The English – and Scottish – fascination with the glories of Scotland, past and present, had begun. It was cemented in 1869 when Queen Victoria herself took a steamer trip along the loch, and later bought a house on the shore.

Mike Kreis, the team's mentor at the loch, advises Blowfish, Charlie and Jay on the 'watercraft'. There is less food here because it's a reservoir, and much 'cleaner' than normal. ('Green water' gives you more bait fish.) Pike are usually ambush predators – here they have had to adapt their natural behaviour and hunt, as there are fewer fish. And there are fewer sunken trees in the water that might serve as ambush points. Pike generally spawn here in April – by January they'll have started checking out likely spawning grounds, in shallower water. The larger pike tend to be scavengers, so dead bait – trout – is the best bet.

The water in the loch is 3°C; pike are a little less active in cold water, but they will feed. Mike suggests that the boys fish at a 'drop-off', a shelf between deep and shallow water. The steamship is likely to frighten away any fish, so the team now take to an old-fashioned rowing boat. How to catch them? Jay has had an idea: he'll take to a 'para-motor', a powered para-glider, so he can quickly 'chum' a large area of water in the middle of the loch, otherwise inaccessible, by dropping the bait in from 30 metres up in the sky.

This bizarre method actually works. Back on the boat, Jay is the first to hook. A decent-sized pike is reeled in, and this is where they are a real hazard. As Blowfish points out, pike can have up to 700 teeth, and they aren't shy about using them: this brute takes its revenge by biting Charlie on the hand. Pike have an anti-coagulant in their saliva – so their prey will bleed to death if they manage to escape. Charlie's fairly confident he will survive: but his cut will bleed all day – a pike-fishing souvenir he won't relish.

The brown trout were off limits in Loch Katrine, so the team have now come to try for some in a very different kettle of fish: Howietoun Fishery trout ponds. The brown trout that have been bred here are world-famous; since 1881 their eggs have been exported all over the globe. Here, the team are planning to hone their winter-fishing techniques.

Due to the cold weather, the trout aren't going to be moving around too much: the bait has to be dropped right in front of their noses. Jay, still obsessed with flight-fishing, challenges Blowfish and Charlie to use a children's box kite to manoeuvre the bait on a line right into the middle of the trout pond, so they can fish in a far larger area than would be accessible by rod and line.

To everyone's surprise, after a few aborted efforts, the kite works. Thanks to Charlie's navigation skills, Blowfish manages to lower the hook into the water, bring the kite up again, and catch a trout.

But Jay trumps the humble kite with a state of the art drone, exactly the kit that's been used to get the aerial shots for *Fishing Impossible*. It's not as easy as it looks – Ollie the cameraman has spent a considerable amount of time learning how to fly it; Jay only has an hour. He does get to grips with it, after a fashion, but he fails to catch any trout, only weed. Old technology is the victor here.

The Howietoun experiment shows that dropping an airborne hook right next to the mouths of semi-dormant, wintering fish does work. But as neither the kite nor the drone will survive in the middle of a stormy Scapa Flow, how will they do it in Orkney?

To get used to the kind of rough seas they'll encounter, Charlie has headed ninety miles east, to Usan, on the Scottish coast near Montrose. He'll be fishing, with his favoured rod and line, for Atlantic cod, which are active during the winter months, but extremely challenging to catch.

CHARLIE:
'WINTER COD FISHING IS RENOWNED AMONG FISHERMEN EVERYWHERE FOR BEING SOME OF THE TOUGHEST, BUT MOST REWARDING FISHING YOU CAN DO.'

From October to February the cod come in from the deep North Sea to feed along the Scottish coast. The rough waters stir up the sea bed and they can find worms, crustaceans and small fish – cod are not fussy eaters. In the summer they hunt by sight; in the winter, by scent.

Charlie has gone to the top here for local knowledge – he's fishing with Mike Horn, a Scottish international fisherman and Chairman of the Scottish Federation of Sea Anglers. The main bait they'll be using is a delicacy irresistible to the cod, 'peeler' crab. It's so known because the crab is caught just as it starts the periodic shedding of its hard shell. That's then peeled off, leaving the soft flesh underneath. Peelers are hunted in the autumn and frozen as bait.

The fishing isn't easy: after several hours of casting away from a rock precariously placed above the fierce waves, nothing has been caught. But then the tide starts to ebb: magic hour.

With night falling, Charlie and the team carefully clamber out 100 metres over the slippery rocks and kelp. In the dark, at the mercy of the raging North Sea, this is one place you really don't want to fall over.

FACT FILE COD LEVELS

The 'Cod Wars' between Britain and Iceland were a regular feature of the 1970s. Today, there is still a cod war raging – now, it is caused by 'discard' fishing. If a trawler has a licence to catch 10 tonnes of crab, say, but ends up netting 5 tonnes of cod, then the fish are simply thrown back, dead, into the water. Currently, this wasteful practice is permissible by international law. But after determined lobbying, led by Hugh Fearnley-Whittingstall and others, and supported by Mike's federation, the EU has at last voted to ban the practice.

The Scottish sea angling clubs don't neglect sustainable fishing here on their doorstep. Only adult cod measuring more than 35cm in length are allowed to be put into the fishing bags and brought up to be weighed during a competition. Anything under this size is released straight away. Large hooks are used so as to minimize the risk of the smaller whiting, or juvenile cod, being caught. And over the last year or two, there have been some encouraging signs here, with anglers noticing an increased number of younger fish. As Mike puts it, 'Nature has a great way of replenishing itself if we leave it alone for a little while.'

CHARLIE:
'THIS IS SOME FISHING SPOT: WE'VE GOT HUGE BREAKERS CRASHING IN ON US NOW, I MEAN IT REALLY IS AN EXTREME PLACE TO FISH. YOU'RE JUST EXPOSED OUT ON THIS ROCKY HEADLAND, IT'S REALLY HARDCORE.'

But, with the necessary safety measures in place, early evening at ebb tide offers quite the best conditions in which to catch the Atlantic cod, as they swim into the deeper gullies and channels in search of food. And all this travail is worth it: Charlie catches a decent cod, around 1.5 kilos in weight.

Jay and Blowfish have been fishing at the other end of the spectrum from Charlie, in the far gentler waters of the River Annan. A small river, fifty miles long, in Dumfries and Galloway, it reaches the sea at the Solway Firth, the border between Scotland and England. The Annan is renowned for its fly-fishing, and especially its wild brown trout. It's close season on salmon and trout in the river

now, but fishing for grayling is still on. Like the pike in Loch Katrine, they're an introduced species – they only arrived in Annan at the end of the nineteenth century. And yet, ironically, for a long while the owners of trout streams like this one regarded grayling as a pest, and did their best to eradicate them. In recent years, though, they've found increasing favour with dedicated anglers. They're now regarded as the fourth game fish, after salmon, brown trout and sea trout, and are known charmingly as the 'Queen of the River', or the 'Lady of The Stream'.

Jay and Blowfish have come here to try out a technique which is very effective for catching fish in cold, winter rivers: 'Czech nymphing'. A nymph in this context is a fly at an early stage of its development, and a method of fishing that imitates its movements has become immensely popular in the Czech Republic in recent years. It's a technique designed for fishing on the riverbed, and it's particularly well suited to grayling, whose natural habitat this is. The current is weaker, requiring less effort on the part of both the fish, and the flies on which they feed.

The idea is to cast upstream and allow the artificial nymph to sink gently to the bottom and drift past the angler. The Czech nymph is made heavy enough to be able to fall to the riverbed at the same pace as a real one would. No external weights are attached, nor is a float used. A grayling's bite is a gentle nibble – any suspicion of it and the rod is raised up sharply.

If it works in the Vltava, it's surely going to work here. But, after several hours, patience is wearing thin. Jay's been dutifully casting upstream and dragging the 'bug' along the bottom, but has caught nothing.

The grayling don't range widely in the cold water, but tend to stick to one place, in a shoal, where they can best feed without wasting too much energy. So it's a case of patiently repeating the process over and over again, gradually moving upstream until the grayling can be found.

This isn't for everyone: those outside the fishing community can't always understand the appeal. As the great American comedian Steven Wright once put it, 'There's a fine line between fishing and just standing on the shore like an idiot.' But patience and perseverance are the prime assets of the assiduous angler. And, as so often, they pay off. Jay lands a beautiful, red-finned, red-banded grayling.

So now it's crunch time – the evening before the last day, and Jay, Charlie and Blowfish are back together. A ferry ride – one of the most notoriously rough crossings in the British Isles – takes them from Scrabster, just over 30 kilometres away from John o' Groats, to Stromness, on the south-west coast of 'Mainland' island – Orkney's biggest, as the name suggests.

The larger Orkney islands were inhabited at least 8,500 years ago; by the Iron Age they were a stronghold of the Picts; in AD 875 they fell to the Vikings. From the late fifteenth century, the islands have been under Scottish sovereignty – but many Norse words survive in the Orcadian dialect.

Historically, the strategic importance of Orkney lies not in its islands, but in its great natural harbour, Scapa Flow. The name is derived from the Norse, *Skalpaflói* – bay of the long isthmus.

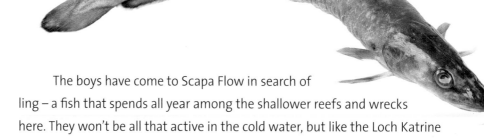

The boys have come to Scapa Flow in search of ling – a fish that spends all year among the shallower reefs and wrecks here. They won't be all that active in the cold water, but like the Loch Katrine pike, they can be caught – with sufficient patience, and cunning.

At Scapa Flow, as at Howietoun and Annan, Jay's plan is to put the bait right in front of the fishes' mouths. And to do this they need to dive down to see where the fish are hiding. Scuba diving among wrecks, though, is fraught with danger. As Blowfish, a qualified divemaster, points out.

FACT FILE SCAPA FLOW

In 1903 Erskine Childers, a high-ranking Anglo-Irish civil servant (and, later, gun-runner in the cause of Irish independence), published what became one of the first great classics of the spy adventure genre, *The Riddle of the Sands*. The aim of publishing it wasn't just to offer a rip-snorting yarn: its real purpose was to sway public opinion against Admiralty policy, which was still organizing the United Kingdom's naval defences with the age-old enemy, France, in mind. Childers and others realized that after the Kiel Canal joined the Baltic to the North Sea, in 1895, giving the German Navy direct access to the latter, the main threat to the Kingdom's security came from that ever-increasing German Navy, not the French. And yet: 'We have no naval base in the North Sea, and no North Sea Fleet. Our best battleships are too deep in draught for North Sea work.'

This advocacy paid off – a new breed of warship was developed for deployment in the North Sea. Scapa Flow became the main harbour for this fleet. 'Block ships' were sunk so as to provide a series of underwater barriers. Vessels based here took part in some of the most decisive battles of both world wars, including the Battle of Jutland, in 1916, the pivotal naval engagement of the First World War.

And then came one of the most bizarre incidents in naval history. In accord with the Armistice signed in November 1918, seventy-four ships from the Imperial High Seas Fleet arrived in Scapa Flow for internment. Just over six months later, owing to a mistaken belief that still-ongoing negotiations had failed, the German commander decided to scuttle the fleet, rather than allowing it to fall into what he still regarded as enemy hands. Fifty-two ships were sunk – the greatest loss of shipping ever recorded in a single day. All but seven have since been brought to the surface.

In October 1939, a month after the Second World War had begun, HMS *Ark Royal* was torpedoed and sunk by a German submarine while lying at anchor in the harbour, with the loss of 833 lives. Before this, the Navy had considered Scapa Flow impregnable. The First Lord of the Admiralty, one Winston Churchill, now took matters in hand and had a series of barriers built around the harbour – a phenomenal exercise in military engineering later named after its sponsor.

Jay has a personal reason for coming here: his grandfather served on the cruiser HMS *Norfolk*, which was based in Scapa Flow. In 1943 he narrowly avoided personal disaster when she came under fire after engaging the German battleship *Scharnhorst*. The *Scharnhorst* was sunk – a major victory in the Arctic Campaign. Jay, of course, continued in the family tradition – as a Royal Marine Commando.

BLOWFISH:

'YOU WILL BE SWIMMING AROUND SOMETHING THAT WILL HAVE HUGE, JAGGED, SHARP PIECES OF METAL. IF IT CATCHES YOUR DRY SUIT, YOU'LL FILL IT WITH WATER IN SECONDS. NOT ONLY WILL YOU BE FREEZING TO DEATH, YOU WILL BE NEGATIVELY BUOYANT, AND YOU WON'T COME BACK UP.'

To stay safe, Jay will be diving in tandem with Blowfish. Jay will hold the rod and reel; Blowfish, with the line threaded through ties on a long wooden pole, will present the bait right up to the fish.

For Charlie, though, less experienced in scuba diving, this is a risk too far, so he won't be going underwater with them. He's not at a loose end: after getting in touch with a local angling club, he scours the island for fishing rods, picking up a haul of twenty. While Jay and Blowfish are going for pinpoint accuracy, Charlie is going to be in a boat covering as much water as he can; each rod will have four hooks. Not all the fish will be hiding in the wrecks – Charlie is aiming to catch any that might swim by. When he explains the idea to Jay and Blowfish they are far from impressed, and supremely confident that they will be the ones catching tonight's supper. Game on.

JAY:

'IT'S LIKE DIVING DOWN INTO THE ABYSS.
ALL OF A SUDDEN YOU START TO FEEL VERY VULNERABLE.'

Out to sea, Jay and Blowfish go over the side and pass down through the eerie green waters, a surreal netherworld of long-forgotten warrior ships five fathoms deep, ghostly sentinels now stationed on the seabed. They settle by the wreck of the SMS *(Seiner Majestät Schiff) V83*, a destroyer scuttled in 1919, only three years after she was launched in Hamburg. Once a proud 84 metres long, she now lies in two rusting and marine-encrusted sections.

Blowfish and Jay, of course, haven't just dived in without trying out their ingenious rod and pole combination. It was rigorously tested the evening before, for a whole five minutes as they enjoyed a drink in the bar, and passed with flying colours. Underwater, it's a different story. The line, now at the mercy of the current, seems to manage to catch itself on every single edge, nook and cranny. This would be a problem even if they were fishing from up top in the conventional

THE BLOWFISH FILE

ORKNEY FISH IN WINTER

The fish are waiting out the winter. Because of the cold, their metabolic rates are low, giving them less energy to move about. And because they're not trying to get into condition to breed, there's no great need for them to feed.

The winter seas around Scapa Flow are dangerous and temperamental, and conditions can change on a knife edge. Storms create turbulence which churns up the water and lowers visibility, so the fish are in danger of being forced into dangerous bays, beached, or smashed against the rocks. Bigger fish tend to move to the deeper ocean, where conditions are stable all year round. Smaller fish don't follow them – because then they'd just become prey themselves. Instead they seek safety hiding away under the wrecks, not doing too much, and waiting for it all to blow over. Come spring and the plankton bloom, there's food everywhere and the cycle will begin again.

manner. Down here it's plain dangerous: if Jay and Blowfish snag themselves on the hook it could tear one of the suits. Blowfish has no choice but to cut the line.

But these boys are not quitters: Plan B is for Jay to man the rod in a rubber dinghy on the surface while Blowfish, with only the pole and bait to contend with, swims up to a wreck and pokes it in. He can see that there are fish hiding among the hulks.

Charlie, with his array of rods set up, is far from confident – the cold water is going to seriously limit his chances of catching a ling. And there seems to be far more activity on the boat than in the water beneath it. Keeping check on the rods is like spinning plates: Charlie has to keep crawling under or hurdling the forest of rods every time he thinks he has a bite – and he gets there too late to reel them in.

Blowfish and Jay's confidence, as it turns out, was misplaced; the fish are in the wrecks all right, but they're just not interested in feeding. The boys have to face the facts. Wearily downcast, they call it a day and make their way back to the mothership. There's one consolation: at least Charlie won't have done any better with his old-fashioned plethora of rods.

But what's this? Charlie serves up a fish wrap, ling, cooked on board and caught on one of the previously derided rods while Blowfish and Jay were down in the watery depths.

As the ling wraps go down, the cold recedes from the team's bones, and the mental agony begins to fade, the benefits of catching at least one fish for supper, whatever the method, overcome the disappointment of Jay and Blowfish's dive.

NORWAY

THE LOCATION: NORWAY

THE QUARRY: RED KING CRAB

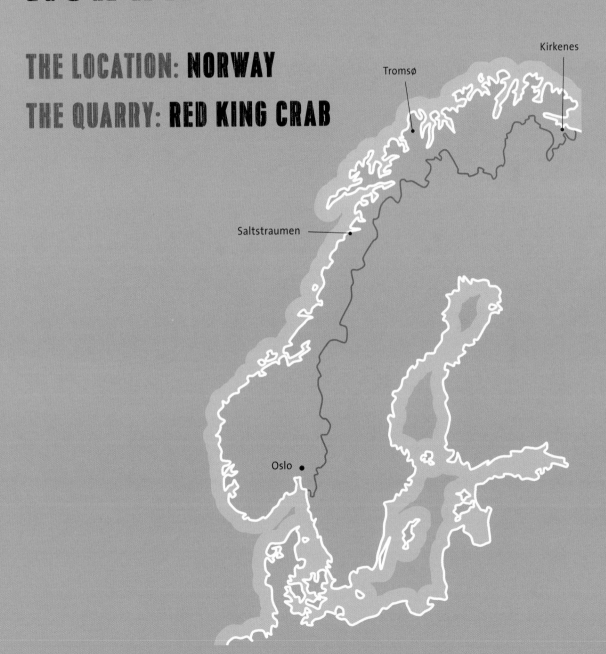

Kirkenes

Tromsø

Saltstraumen

Oslo

BLOWFISH IS A VIKING. Hird, his family name, denotes the standard-bearers to the Norse kings, the armed escort, the fighters. And so it's not a huge surprise that his challenge to Charlie and Jay is to fish in Scandinavia. But this is going to be a challenge that even the Vikings might have found too much. The team are going to fish in the far north of Norway, in the Arctic Circle, in the middle of winter, in temperatures that reach as low as –30°C, and where daylight lasts just a few hours.

On their journey up to Europe's most northerly point, the boys are going to be fishing a mere sprint away from the world's strongest whirlpool, and trying to catch fish through a hole in the ice, guided by the Sami and watched by a herd of bemused reindeer. Then the *pièce de résistance*: diving, in freezing water, for the ultra-tasty red king crab. Growing up to almost 2 metres across, claw to claw, this is a fearsome warrior in itself. And Blowfish is planning to catch one by hand.

'Viking' is a catch-all term to describe medieval Scandinavians on tour, rather than peacefully at home in the kingdoms of Denmark, Norway and Sweden. And they were keen travellers: over three centuries they attacked, and settled in, Britain, Ireland, Iceland, Greenland, Canada, Russia, Normandy and southern Italy. They also raided the French and Iberian seaboards and, via the River Volga, the Caspian and Black Seas. They were even present in Constantinople – where they served in the Byzantine emperor's crack Varangian Guard.

Norway is one of Europe's most mountainous countries – for more than 400 million years it's been strewn with them. As long as 10,000 years ago, the ice sheet that covered the country began to melt, forming fjords, lakes, rivers and as many as 50,000 islands. Thick forests grew up in place of most of the tundra.

The first outing, once the team arrive, is a boat ride off Saltstraumen, on the north-west coast of Norway, just inside the Arctic Circle. More than a pleasure trip, this introduces them to the truly bizarre nature of the water in the area: the Saltstraumen Strait turns out to be the most powerful tidal water anywhere in the world. Every six hours, 400 million cubic metres of ice-cold water barrel through the narrow channel, 150 kilometres long and 3 kilometres deep, at speeds of up to 25mph. This tumult creates a 'maelstrom', whirlpools up to 10 metres in diameter and 5 metres deep; powerful enough to suck small boats into their maws. The key to the boys' survival in these waters is that their craft is a rubber-hulled inflatable, with a powerful motor; even so, the giant eddy manages to spin it 90 degrees as it sails through, such is the sheer force of the current.

'Maelstrom' literally means millstream, but that hardly does it justice; a crushing current would be nearer the mark. The original one from which the term is borrowed is at Moskstraumen, 100 miles north-west of Saltstraumen, in the Lofoten archipelago. It was put on the map in 1841 by Edgar Allen Poe in his short story 'A Descent into the Maelström'. Thirty years later, Jules Verne also featured a deadly vortex, into which Captain Nemo deliberately drives the *Nautilus,* at the gripping conclusion of *20,000 Leagues Under the Sea.*

Next day the fun starts in earnest as the boys are sent out by Blowfish to get used to the Arctic conditions. There's a particular pleasure in store for Charlie. Blowfish wants to toughen him up, ready for the rigours ahead. Blowfish assumes that Jay, as a former Commando, will be up to scratch. Never mind that Charlie's leisure time, when he's not fly-fishing, is spent shinning up mountains on 100-kilometre runs: this doesn't come anywhere near meeting Blowfish's exacting standards of peak physical condition. The idea behind this is that when Blowfish disappears under the ice in search of the king crab, he needs a lineman, someone to hold the all-important lifeline, without losing concentration in the cold. Unbeknown to Charlie, this is his audition for the role. Blowfish wants to get him used to fishing in the extreme conditions, and so, while Jay and Blowfish are going to be doing so from the safety of a comfortable, modern powerboat, with the most sophisticated tackle money can buy, Charlie is consigned to hand-lining in a kayak. Blowfish has, though, relented to the extent of allowing him a total immersion wet suit. He's going to need it.

FACT FILE **SKREI**

The prize cod catch off Norway is undoubtedly *skrei*, the name given to cod caught as they migrate from the Barents Sea – the largest concentration of Atlantic cod in the world. Between January and April they come westwards down the coast of Norway to their spawning grounds. Skrei – the name derives from a Norse word meaning *wanderer* – is so valued that it has to have a special certificate when offered for sale. The local notion is that the fish's migration tones up its brilliant white, low-fat, nutritious and flaky, melt-in-the-mouth flesh.

The north-east Arctic cod stock is managed jointly by Norway and Russia. A whole catalogue of regulations is in place, dictating the minimum size of cod that can be caught, restricting the density of trawlers' nets, and outlawing the discard of cod that's been caught unintentionally. It seems to be working: according to government figures the north-east Arctic cod stock is estimated to be four times larger than it was two or three decades ago.

Cod, once dried, is 80% protein, and this dried and salted version has been a Norwegian staple, and export, for more than five centuries. Fresh or dried, cod has always been considered far superior to local pretenders such as haddock and pollock. Given the recent pressure on cod numbers, though, haddock has recently become far more common in our fish and chip shops and supermarkets.

The team take to the waters off the Saltstraumen coast, with its desolate stark landscape, blanketed with snow, strewn with clusters of green and purple trees. A visitor might assume that fish would keep well away from a maelstrom, only a few hundred yards off. But the water, even a few dozen metres from the coastline, is already deep. This suits cod, pollock, wolffish, haddock, and halibut – now a very rare fish indeed – all of which, the local anglers assure the boys, are just waiting to be caught. That's good – or there's no supper.

But the fish don't want to make this easy. A big one hooked by Blowfish snaps his line with ease. Jay hooks as well and pumps the rod up and down as he reels in, playing the fish. He lands a haddock – but it's not big enough to feed three hungry men and so it's let go.

In his unstable kayak, Charlie is finding it hard to manipulate the hand-line – not least because his hands are freezing, even with gloves. But Blowfish has been indulgent enough to allow Charlie several hooks, and he manages to catch three pollock – again, too small to eat, so back they go.

The problem here in Saltstraumen is that there are only five hours of daylight in January – sunset is at 3 o'clock in the afternoon. And fishing right next to the strongest tidal current in the world, if you were advised to do it at all, is not something you'd want to do in the dark. So Charlie is now released from his labours. Jay and Blowfish, though, are able to carry on fishing in their well-appointed powerboat. By 4 o'clock in the afternoon it's already pitch black.

But then Jay catches one of the star fish of the whole series, a huge Atlantic cod. The average size is around a kilo, Blowfish points out; this monster turns out to be 17 kilos. Charlie, on being allowed on to the boat, drops to his knees: 'I thought he'd got hold of a dummy.' Not only will it feed the three boys; it will feed the entire crew.

JAY:
'DEARIE ME, LOOK AT THE SIZE OF THAT, IT'S CODZILLA.
THE BIGGEST COD I'VE EVER SEEN, LET ALONE CAUGHT.'

A successful day having come to an end, Charlie and Blowfish relax in what Charlie calls 'true Norwegian fashion' – in a steaming hot tub, fringed with lanterns, and surrounded by snow. Jay cooks the cod on an open fire, just as our Stone Age ancestors would have done: 'If you ever taste a cod like that,' Jay reckons, 'you'll never want fish and chips in the UK again.'

The next day, the team head further into the frozen north, past rocks fringed with fingers of water frozen in its tracks, a spun-sugar ice cascade. They're going to an area south of Tromsø to meet the Sami, the nomadic tribe who used to be known to the English as the Lapps, or Laplanders, now regarded as a pejorative term. The northernmost indigenous people in Europe, the Sami are hardy, tough and resourceful. They have learned over more than fifty centuries how to survive, and thrive, in the extremely harsh winters. Nowadays the Sami use powered snowmobiles and GPS apps to herd their reindeer. But they still revere their old ways of living, fishing techniques included.

FACT FILE **THE SAMI**

The *Sápmi* region – around 390,000 square kilometres – stretches across northern Norway, Sweden and Finland and the Kola peninsula, in north-west Russia. Although their genetic history is not fully understood, the Sami would seem to be unrelated to Norwegians, Swedes, Finns or Russians.

In prehistory the Sami began as reindeer hunters, but around AD 1500 they gradually turned into reindeer herders. They still practise transhumance – following the herd as it moves between summer and winter pastures. They're the last European people leading a subsistence lifestyle. Sami in the coastal areas are mostly engaged in fishing. Only around 10% of the tribe today, the 'Mountain Sami' as opposed to the 'Sea Sami', are reindeer herders.

There are now only between 60,000 and 100,000 Sami. The wide discrepancy in the figures is because in recent times many Sami have either chosen, or been forced, to desert their traditional nomadic culture. Encroachment on to their historic lands seems to be an unstoppable tide. Their winter pasture lands are down by almost half; reindeer numbers are falling.

The threats are legion. In part they come from the usual suspects: government projects to build roads, tunnels and power lines; military ranges carved out for bombing practice; logging; the building of hydro-electric dams; open-cast mining, which not only takes over their land but also dumps toxic chemicals into the fjords; radioactive waste and spent nuclear fuel (a Russian contribution, as was Chernobyl, which made its effects known here). But now the Sami, like many indigenous peoples across the world confronted with 'progress', are becoming politically active, determined to fight their corner.

The boys have come to the Mauken reindeer herding region. Nils Oskal, who will be their main guide – and protector – kits them out with traditional Sami costume. No Gore-Tex here, but thick, warming coats made of reindeer fur. The hairs of reindeer pelt are naturally configured so as to form a honeycomb of air chambers – the best insulation of any clothing known to mankind until the synthetics developed as a by-product of the Space Age. And they're going to be needed, Nils points out. You would very quickly freeze to death in your day clothes up in the mountains where the Sami are taking the team to fish. The temperature could be anything between –15° and –40°C.

The best way to get out there across the sheer ice and snowdrifts is by sled or snowmobile. The team opt for the motorized transport and then it's time to get to grips with one of the most traditional fishing methods of the Arctic world: ice fishing. The boys have to cut a hole in the ice, using an 'ice auger' – a giant corkscrew operated by a rotary handle. It's drilled through ice a metre thick until a big enough hole is made, ready to drop a line through into the waters below.

Then the rods the boys will be using are handed out. They are only around 30cm long, and between 15 and 20cm from the tiny, toy-like reel to the tip. While it might seem ridiculous, the tiny 'jigging' rod is just what's needed for fishing over a small aperture in the ice, over which a conventional rod would be unwieldy and useless.

After hours waiting in the snow, nothing has been caught. It's so cold that the water on Jay's fishing line freezes solid. But suddenly he strikes, and reels up a little Arctic char, a beauty with a red tail and red undercarriage. This, Blowfish tells him, is a salmonid, a relative of the salmon and trout, and the most northern-dwelling freshwater fish anywhere in the world – it needs the extremely cold water to thrive.

And with the fishing completed, there is another treat in store, the Aurora Borealis, the Northern Lights. In Norse mythology they were believed to be reflections from the shields of the Valkyries, the women warriors charged by Odin to guide fallen heroes to Valhalla. They've certainly made one honorary Viking's day.

BLOWFISH:
'STANDING UP HERE, ON TOP OF THE WORLD, ON A FROZEN ICE LAKE, STARING AT THE NORTHERN LIGHTS ... NORWAY IS AWESOME.'

The next morning it's time to leave Mauken and head up to Tromsø. Nearly 220 miles north of the Arctic Circle, it's reckoned to be the most northerly city in the world. An important fishing port and centre for Arctic trade, it's crammed on to the island of Tromsøya, surrounded by pristine white mountains and startling blue seas. In the eighteenth and nineteenth centuries, Tromsø was known as 'the Paris of the North'. You can see why: many attractive wooden houses still stand along its elegant streets. In the early twentieth century the Arctic expeditions of Amundsen, Nansen and others were inaugurated, recruited and trained here. You can feel why: average January temperatures are below –4°C. The *Fishing Impossible* team, taking a cue from the illustrious Arctic explorers of the past, are also going to use Tromsø as a place to acclimatize further. Extreme conditions will await them when they come to rendezvous with the red king crab.

The boys have chartered a handsome wooden sailing boat to take them fishing, the *Biskop Hvoslef*, built in 1932, a lifeboat now used for 'whale safaris'. It's a common misconception, Blowfish points out, that cold water means less life; the opposite is the case – cold water has more oxygen, and more nutrients than warm water. That's proved half a mile out to sea when a pair of stately humpback whales put in an appearance. Humpbacks had been hunted to the point of extinction, but since they were made a protected species their numbers have slowly recovered – there are now around 80,000 across the world. And then there's an even rarer sight – a pod of orcas. The orca – or 'killer whale' – is far more common in the southern hemisphere; Jay, Charlie and Blowfish are extremely lucky to see them here off the coast of Norway, where there might only be around 500 in residence.

The seas, fjords, lakes and rivers here – in contrast to some of the other parts of the world that *Fishing Impossible* has tried its luck in – are vibrant with life. And that's not an accident – it's the result of careful stewardship, which, once finally put in place, has drawn the waters here back from the brink.

NORWAY ECOLOGY

The Norwegians realized very early on how important their fish stocks were, and, unlike pretty much every other government on the planet, they listened to their scientists. And they've reaped the rewards because of it. Norwegian fish stocks are epic. They have large fish and plenty of them. The presence of orcas indicates just how rich these seas really are.

Global warming and carbon emissions are another story; but if every government listened to scientific recommendations for what level of fishing is sustainable, the problem would pretty much solve itself within five years. But that's not profitable for the fisheries.

The sighting of whales is a doubly good omen; they are here because their prey are here; follow the whales and you will find the fish. But there's another challenge for Charlie. As lineman he may need to dive in if Blowfish gets into difficulties. Would he be able to cope with the freezing temperatures? Cold water can disorientate and confuse a diver, and indecision can be fatal. So Blowfish decides that he and Charlie are going to fish, in the freezing cold, stripped down to their underpants. Whether they have stumbled on an important breakthrough in fishing techniques can't at this early stage be determined for sure. But soon three pollock are hooked: two for Blowfish, one – cold comfort – for Charlie.

The time has come for the culmination of the trip, and a far harder challenge – the hunt for the red king crab. Blowfish, Jay and Charlie drive east across the frozen Arctic landscape towards Kirkenes, on the north-east coast of Norway, 250 miles into the Arctic Circle. Kirkenes is located on the Varangerfjord, the most easterly in Norway, 9 kilometres from the Russian border. Here to the north and east is the Barents Sea. Russian waters, though that's strongly disputed by the Norwegians, not least because of the presence of oil.

At daybreak on the final day, snow powder is swirling around in the wind like the vapours of a Jekyll and Hyde potion. Here, the mountains that run through Norway flatten out into a plateau of polar tundra. Motorized vehicles are no use, so the boys take to two sleds, pulled by ferocious-looking huskies across the frozen fjord. When they get out, they're walking on top of the Arctic Ocean.

In peak fishing season in the autumn most king crabs are caught commercially, with traps. It can be dangerous, even fatal work, given the icy conditions out at sea. The quickest and surest way to catch one at this time of year is to go out onto the ice, dive into the water and take one by hand. That's hardly risk-free either, but it's what Blowfish is aiming to do. And it's why Jay and Charlie – along with a safety team specially flown in – are geared up to make sure that having dived in, he comes back up.

We know why the team are here; but what about the crabs? They're here only because in the 1960s Russian 'scientists' decided it would be a good idea, because the king crab is large and full of good-tasting meat, to round up a posse of them in their home in Kamchatka – some 3,000 miles away, on the Pacific coast – and introduce them into the Barents and White Seas, around Murmansk.

They soon made themselves at home. A voracious eater with no predators in its new berth – the classic hallmark of the invasive species – the red king crab munches its way through crustaceans at a rate of knots, so that some native species have all but disappeared. Fish eggs are another favourite snack – and it's feared that it may be eating up those of the capelin, a small forage fish that is one of the main staples of the Atlantic cod. And there's plenty of pressure on cod numbers already.

THE RED KING CRAB

In order to grow, a king crab might moult – shed its shell – twenty times during its lifetime. Just before it starts moulting it begins to absorb sea water, which helps it crack open the hard shell – the exoskeleton – that's tightly packed around it. Once the shell has broken, the animal pulls itself out of the old carapace. Then it might take on up to a third of its weight again in water, becoming swollen like a sponge. Once fully engorged with sea water, the animal starts to re-harden its soft carapace, becoming fully armoured once again. This time, though, two-thirds crab, one-third sea water are enclosed within the shell, and during the intermoult period the crab replaces this sea water with flesh as it once again grows to bursting point within its exoskeleton. Breeding can only take place after moulting, when the genital pores on females are open and able to accept sperm.

The Norwegian authorities, meanwhile, are caught in a pincer movement. Do they carry on applying their usual, effective fish resource management techniques, and protect the king crab? Or do they declare war on it? Because of its great value to fishermen, restaurants and food retailers, not too many people are all that keen to see its numbers radically reduced. And that's not good news: it's already spreading westwards along the Norway coast and some ecologists worry that it might end up buffeting its way as far as Gibraltar.

Blowfish, Charlie, Jay and the dive safety team arrive at the crab fishing grounds. A Blowfish-sized hole is going to have to be dug out of the ice, which is a half metre thick. And they've only got about two hours of daylight to do that – and dive for the king crab. The hole is going to be triangular: straight sides are easier to clamber out of if Blowfish needs to make an emergency exit from the water.

And so while Charlie and Jay – the warriors of the king – stand guard, Blowfish himself struggles into a special type of dry suit especially designed for diving in extremely cold temperatures. Even so, he will soon lose body heat under the ice and has a maximum of ten minutes to be in the water. This is where all the teamwork is going to be at a premium.

Jay is on comms, Charlie is the wingman, holding on to the lifeline – all that links Blowfish to safety. With a powerful torch, Blowfish submerges into the disorienting gloom. It's almost pitch black, except for the white ceiling of ice shining tantalizingly above him. Blowfish drifts towards the seabed where the king crab will be quietly stumbling along, depopulating the marine life.

But then, disaster. Blowfish finds he can't 'equalize'. This is one of the most common problems when a diver descends. Diving to any significant depth can cause pain in the ears. (If you've never dived, think of the unpleasant sensation you may have experienced while coming in to land on an aeroplane.) Underwater, not only is it far more painful, it can be dangerous. Burst an eardrum and not only will you bleed profusely, it can cause permanent and debilitating damage to the ear, not least deafness. To prevent this you need to increase the pressure in your middle ear – which is usually dead air – to equalize it with the outer ear and the space around you. To do that you need to allow air to pass through your Eustachian tubes, thin tubes connecting the mouth with the ear. The most usual

method is to pinch your nose and gently blow air down into it. The increase in pressure then forces air up your Eustachian tubes and thus equalizes the pressure between the middle and outer ear.

It's not always as easy as it sounds – and it's especially difficult if you're wearing a 'full face mask', as Blowfish is doing in his dive for the king crab. They're designed so you can pinch your nose from the outside, but if the mask is tight, as his proves to be, it's extremely hard to achieve. And when things start to go wrong underwater, even for the most experienced diver a chain reaction of stress can set in.

And there's a more immediate danger: uneven pressure in the middle ear can disorientate a diver so that he's unable to make clear decisions, especially as stress and anxiety levels rise. He could easily swim away from the ice hole and not towards it. And if Blowfish blacks out and gets trapped under the ice, no amount of Charlie's tugging on the rope will save him.

Blowfish tries to descend again, hoping that his ear will clear. But it's no good, it doesn't – in fact the pain gets worse – and he has to come back up out of the water. This is a genuine crisis: the whole mission might have to be abandoned. The finest king crab on the planet is not worth risking your health for, let alone your life.

But the team have come so far to do this; Blowfish isn't going to give up now. He goes back into the water. This will have to be the last attempt. The pain soon returns, and it looks like he's going to have to give up after all. But then he suddenly spots something ambling along the seabed: a huge red king crab.

Blowfish has had many crabs through his hands, but not many as big as this; he needs to make sure its lethal claws don't rip his dry suit to shreds. Blowfish makes his move: 'You're coming with me, sunshine.'

BLOWFISH:

'THAT WAS THE BEST DAMN DIVE I'VE EVER DONE IN MY LIFE. WE'VE BAGGED CHAR, WE'VE BAGGED POLLOCK. JAY'S CAUGHT THE BIGGEST COD I'VE EVER SEEN. WE'VE GONE THROUGH RAIN, SLEET, SNOW, ICE, THE WORKS, AND, THE LAST DAY IN NORWAY, WE'VE FINISHED IT OFF WITH THE CROWNING GLORY OF THE KING CRAB.'

PERU

THE LOCATION: **PERU**

THE QUARRY: **HUMBOLDT SQUID**

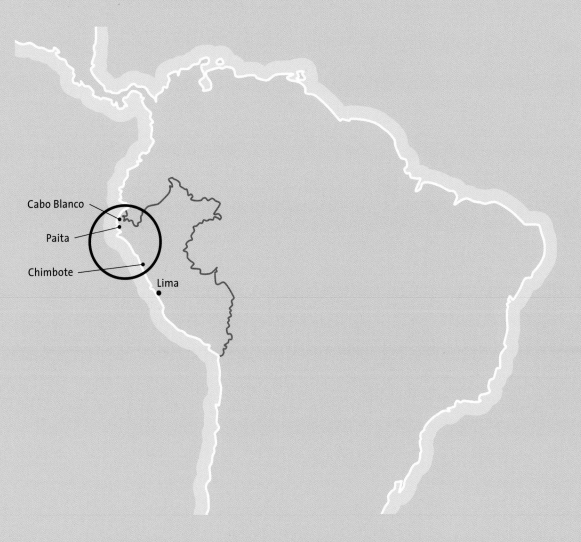

Cabo Blanco

Paita

Chimbote

Lima

THE CHALLENGE

BLOWFISH IS NOT ONLY A MARINE BIOLOGIST but also a qualified divemaster, with all kinds of encounters with extraordinary animals under his belt. But this challenge is going to be something else. He's planning to meet a creature that is as terrifying as it is fascinating, the Humboldt squid, one of the world's largest species. Variously dubbed 'jumbo' or 'flying', as it can propel itself out of the water to evade predators, the species is native to the Eastern Pacific from southern Chile to southern California, and the boys are going to go in search of it in Peru.

This is a serious challenge. The Humboldt squid can camouflage itself, its body changing colour to blend in with the sunlight. It can shoot out ink to confuse or temporarily blind would-be predators, and it can swim at a top speed of 15mph, three times quicker than the quickest human ever recorded. To do this, the squid, like octopuses and other cephalopods, moves through the water using a form of jet propulsion. Water is taken into a cavity in the squid's 'mantle', or torso, then squeezed out of the 'siphon', thus propelling the animal. The mantle, not counting the arms and tentacles, grows up to a metre or more in length, and the squid can weigh over 50 kilos.

The Humboldt squid is perfectly capable of killing divers, although reports of fatalities caused would seem to be anecdotal, fishermen's tales, rather than based on hard facts. Its beak is ferociously powerful; its bite is said to be the strongest on the planet, capable of punching through Kevlar body armour which is twenty times stronger than steel.

Normally, of course, the Humboldt squid is caught by commercial fishermen, with hooks and bait, at as safe a distance as possible – though the squid will fight on to the last. But Blowfish is aiming to swim right up to it, with no weapon of any kind. That's right. One of the most aggressive creatures on the planet and, what's more, one that only comes up to the surface at night.

Peru is twice the size of Texas. This is a country of extremes: its spine is the Andes; to the east is the jungle of the Amazonian rainforest – nearly two-thirds of the country's surface area. The whole coast of north-west Peru, where Blowfish, Jay and Charlie are going to hunt the Humboldt squid, is fringed by desert. But that doesn't mean it has been untouched by human hand. Only in the last forty years or so have archaeologists uncovered a number of ancient sites dating back to the time of the pre-Inca Moche civilization, which flourished between AD 100 and 800 – adobe buildings that are testament to a thriving society that fell into decline around four centuries before that of the Incas got started.

Other impressive ruined sites, dating from later Peruvian civilizations, are also dotted along the north-west coast. The best known are the Valley of the Pyramids; Cajamarca, an important Inca stronghold, the site of a decisive battle won by Pizarro and his Spanish troops in 1532; and the remains of the once fabulous city of Chan Chan.

Arriving at the port of Paita, the boys can see first-hand the crucial importance of fishing in Peru. In terms of the volume of fish landed, it's second in the world's league table, behind China, accounting for nearly 10% of the global catch. And yet the great majority of the Peruvians themselves eat hardly any fish at all. Peru is not a rich nation, especially not in the remote rural areas. Here in Paita the team catch their first glimpse of a Humboldt squid, just unloaded from a fishing boat. And it's easy to see why it's been awarded the appellation 'jumbo'. It's 30–40 kilograms, and Charlie can hardly lift it.

Blowfish shows Jay and Charlie some of its armoury. It's got cupcake-sized eyes, a truly terrifying mouth, and there are tiny little dots all over its body. These are colour-changing cells, called chromatophores. It's now believed that squid flash different colours to each other so as to communicate, possibly to attract mates or warn off rivals. If startled, they can turn from white to red in an instant – which, along with their aggression, gives them their nickname among fishermen, *diablo rojo* – red devil.

More than 400,000 tonnes of squid are caught every year in Peru. The fisherman use light to attract the animals, with a huge spotlight tied to the mast, but the methods they use to catch them are pretty brutal. The boys are shown one of the hooks. It looks like something dating back to medieval warfare, a fearsome object, bristling with vicious-looking spikes, frightening just to look at. A ferocious method of fishing. And exactly the kind of thing that Blowfish is taking so many risks to avoid.

LIGHT

Light is such a driving force in the oceans; even the deep sea is reliant on the daily shift of sun and moon. The 'diurnal vertical migration' is the largest movement of life anywhere on the planet, and it happens every twenty-four hours. Small planktonic life moves down from the ocean surface by day and up towards it at night. These tiny planktonic players are the key ingredient in most oceanic food chains, so where they go, predators follow. At night, the feeding frenzy begins as all animals are attracted to the areas of highest light intensity. Small predators are looking for the dart of tiny crustaceans, while larger predators are attracted by the shimmer of silver moonlight glancing off a smaller fish's body. By introducing an artificial light source, we can hijack this food chain and bring the plankton *and* the predators to us ... and that includes the Humboldt squid.

Blowfish is not going to use bait when he dives to find the squid, so he needs another ruse to attract them towards him. He will be diving down to the depths of the Peruvian seas in a wet suit. Nothing unusual about that. But what is unusual is that he will be decked from head to toe with strings of fairy lights, or, in his words, the very latest in night fishing technology.

There is, as usual, some solid science behind this bizarre outfit. Humboldt squid have exceptional visual predatory skills, and many marine creatures, including those it likes to eat, are attracted to light. This is the stimulation of the food chain that Blowfish is counting on in Peru. Light attracts the squid's supper.

Blowfish outlines his plan to a local fisherman: dive at night and meet the squid, face to face. The reaction is instantaneous: a flood of stories about crewmen falling off boats, being attacked by giant squid and dragged down into the depths, never to be seen or heard from again.

And the news gets worse. It turns out that the boys have come at a bad time. A very bad time. El Niño is throwing its weight around.

During an El Niño year it is mainly the months of December and January that see the worst of the effects. Hence the name: El Niño means 'the boy', but, around Christmas time, specifically the Christ child. El Niño is actually an oscillation – the other side of the coin, when the effects are reversed, is known, naturally enough, as El Niña.

FACT FILE EL NIÑO

An El Niño event takes place at a frequency of between two and seven years, and its effects last around a year; autumn 2015 has seen a quite severe one. Westward-blowing trade winds weaken along the Equator. The changes in pressure and wind speed cause warm surface water to move eastward along the Equator, from the western Pacific to the seaboard of South America. The warm water builds up, or 'thickens', along the coasts of Ecuador, Peru and Chile. This layer of warm water pushes down and prevents the normal upwelling of nutrient and oxygen-rich cold water. Cold water species thus have to move further out to sea in search of it.

Not only does El Niño cause the removal of the fish off the coasts of Peru; it also brings in strong and unpredictable winds – and waves. The boys regroup to consider the new challenge. Blowfish tells them if they want to catch squid they are going to have to look further out to sea. But as Jay points out: 'If we're going a hundred kilometres off the coast we could hit rough weather and big swells. The elements are against us on this one.' Thanks to El Niño, what was dangerous to start with has just seen an extra turn on the ratchet.

BLOWFISH:
'I'M NOT BAILING OUT, BUT THIS IS FAR, FAR BIGGER THAN JUST GOING FOR A BIT OF A SWIM. WE'RE DOING A NIGHT DIVE, SO THAT MAKES EVERYTHING TEN OR FIFTEEN TIMES HARDER AS WELL. SAFETY IS PARAMOUNT. THERE'S NO POINT GOING DOWN IF YOU DON'T COME BACK UP. AND WITH THAT IN MIND I NEED ONE OF YOU GUYS TO BE MY LIFELINE.'

To choose the candidate, Blowfish decides on a test that will result in the survival of the fittest. A test, that is, for Jay and Charlie. The boys will be using traditional Peruvian reef rafts to get out to the best fishing spots offshore. This will require considerable strength and perseverance, because the tide is coming in and the waves are monstrous. They are after mackerel and bonito and they're going to have to catch them with a hand-line, while perched precariously on the raft.

When the Spaniards arrived in Peru in the 1520s and saw the Incas riding the waves on rafts of reed they nicknamed them *'caballitos de totora'* or 'little horses of reed'. The rafts are rather like two logs tied together, with a pointed prow. Here in Peru, it's now believed, lie the ancient origins of the modern surfing obsession. It's easy to see why – to get out to where the fish are, a kilometre or more from shore, you've got to battle across the strong waves. And do the same if you want to get home. Unless you know what you're doing, it's like taking a step backwards for every two forwards.

Charlie and Jay tire quickly fighting the waves, and play their joker by hitching a ride on a motorboat. Jay, having fallen off only once compared to Charlie's six times, gets the job of holding Blowfish's lifeline. In the unpredictable Pacific in an El Niño year, that's a serious responsibility.

While Charlie and Jay have been out testing their mettle, Blowfish has been visiting the laboratory of squid expert Elky Torres. A Humboldt is laid out for him on the slab. 'Damn, that's a big squid!' Like other species, it has eight arms and two longer feeding tentacles. Squid can move the latter faster than the human eye can see. Elky shows Blowfish the suckers – between 100 and 200 on each tentacle – which the squid uses to latch on to its prey. (Which includes members of its own species.) Inside each sucker is a row of sharp 'teeth', which lacerate the flesh of whatever unfortunate creature it's caught. The squid then extends its arms to reel in the prey and drag it into its mouth, where the beak tears it to shreds. And if the tentacles are terrifying enough, the beak is something you really don't want to get too close to.

SQUID BEAKS

The parrot-like beak of the Humboldt squid – hidden inside its mouth – is a miracle of natural engineering. Made from chitin, it's razor-sharp, and far tougher than any man-made synthetic. This lethal set of lips is fully adjustable, allowing the squid to rotate it to the best angle to sample any prey going.

The interesting thing is that if the beak was hard all the way through, then, when the squid bit through a fish, the pressure exerted on one end would cause the beak to dig back into the squid's flesh, like a human trying to hammer in a nail using just their hand. But as the hard, business end of the beak fans up into the soft tissue of the mouth, the beak itself becomes progressively more soft and pliable, and acts as a shock absorber. If we could figure out how squid do that, we could make a huge advance in human orthotics. Put the same technology into people's damaged kneecaps and you've got an absolute winner. Rebuilding knees thanks to squid beaks.

Having been given the most pessimistic assessment of his chances of survival by the local fishermen, Blowfish is hoping that calm, rational science will offer more comfort. Humboldt squid are, he knows, intelligent creatures. As with all marine life, attacks on humans are rare and unlucky. There's no reason to suppose that a squid would go for Blowfish without good cause – fear, surprise, food, territory, mistaken identity. But although some divers have swum along with Humboldt squid and lived to tell the tale, there's no denying that squid do attack divers – on a regular basis. Even Elky, a calm, rational scientist, considers Blowfish's plans for a close encounter with the Humboldt squid crazy. This is not the encouragement Blowfish had been hoping for.

BLOWFISH:

'I'M ABOUT TO GO INTO THE WATER WITH A CANNIBALISTIC, FIFTEEN MILES PER HOUR MISSILE. THIS IS GOING TO BE THE SCARIEST DIVE I'LL EVER DO. I THOUGHT SCIENCE WOULD REASSURE ME MY PLAN IS SOUND, BUT IT'S DONE THE OPPOSITE AND MADE ME EVEN MORE ANXIOUS. I'M NOW BEGINNING TO QUESTION EVERY ASPECT OF THE MISSION.'

efore they head out into the sea on Blowfish's quest, Charlie and Jay cannot resist trying their luck in one of the most legendary fishing locations in recent history, going after one of the most legendary game fish there is. They've come to Cabo Blanco, on Peru's north-west coast, in search of marlin.

Here, there should be optimum fishing conditions: the icy waters of the Humboldt Current collide with warmer water from the Pacific Equatorial Counter-current, bringing millions of plankton to the surface, and stimulating the food chain. So good was the fishing that in the 1950s and 60s Hollywood stars like John Wayne, Humphrey Bogart and Paul Newman – as well as, somewhat incongruously,

---

FACT FILE BIG GAME FISHING

Big game fishing developed around the turn of the twentieth century, made possible by the motorboat. By the 1930s it had become a mini-industry in itself, and assumed its classic form. 'Fighting chairs', rather like those of old-fashioned dental surgeries, and tough harnesses are essential, so powerful are the game fish. So too is heavy tackle – sophisticated rods and wide, strong reels with mechanisms to control the 'drag', or resistance. 'Outriggers' were also developed; poles extended port and starboard, through which the fishing lines are played, thus allowing more lines to be used without them getting tangled when the boat turns.

Marlin, swordfish and sailfish (collectively, billfish), larger tuna (such as yelloweye and bluefin) and sharks (including great white, tiger, hammerhead and mako) – all big, hard-fighting fish – are the most prized quarry. Big game fishing was – and to some extent remains – a rich man's sport. Not only do you need to own, or charter, a fast, powerful, highly manoeuvrable boat, with a crew to drive it and to help with the fishing. The skipper needs to have sufficient knowledge of his seas to identify where the fish might be; he also uses the boat to help drive in the hooks, and help play the fish in – especially if the angler is a novice. A marlin might take a good forty-five minutes to reel in. The main method used once a big fish is hooked is the 'short stroke', a pump and reel action whereby the rod is lifted up around fifteen degrees and, as it's lowered, one turn of the reel is made – or so you hope. In recent decades the eternal mystery of where the fish might be found has been made easier to solve by the use of sonar 'fish finders'.

Marilyn Monroe – came here to catch big fish. The boys can expect to catch blue marlin, which are more frequently taken than black, and yellowfin tuna.

Blowfish, unbeknown to Jay and Charlie, has come to give them some airborne assistance. The idea is to fly over the area of sea where their boat is gamely trolling up and down and help the chaps out by looking for 'bait balls'– groups of smaller fish which are tagging together for protection. It's a big ocean, so if he can give the boys a heads-up as to where smaller fish might be found there's a good chance, or at least some chance, that marlin, swordfish and tuna might also be around. But having flown over the whole area, Blowfish reports that there are no fish to be seen whatsoever. What's more, the rough weather that El Niño trails in its wake has kicked off, causing the wind to change direction rapidly. The resulting huge swells leave Jay and Charlie suffering horribly from seasickness, and with that, it's the end of their expedition.

Warm water brought in by El Niño will have prompted game fish to go further out to sea in search of food, it's true. But El Niño can't be handed all the blame for the lack of fishing here these days. There are other reasons that have nothing to do with natural weather systems.

FACT FILE CABO BLANCO

To say that Cabo Blanco is suffused with faded grandeur would be an understatement. It's a ghost town. Once this was Beverly Hills by the sea; Ernest Hemingway came for an extended stay in 1956, while he was involved in the filming of his novel *The Old Man and the Sea*, starring Spencer Tracy. That book won him the Nobel Prize for Literature, but he landed another prize during his time at Cabo Blanco – a 317kg marlin. That was dwarfed by one caught by Alfred Glassell Jr, the Texas oilman and plutocrat who founded the glamorous and exclusive Cabo Blanco Fishing Club: a massive 707.5kg marlin, 4.5 metres long. That's a record, the largest bony fish ever caught, single-handedly, with rod and reel. And it's one that is likely to stand for a long while yet.

Because those days are over. Simply put, there are no fish.

This is a classic case of overfishing. Not of marlin, nor of the fish they prey on, but of the food that sustained those preyfish. From the late 1960s the commercial fishing community, indulged by the Peruvian government and driven by a burgeoning market for fishmeal (cheap feed for farm animals, exported in huge quantity to Britain, Europe and America), fish oil and bait, thought it might be a good idea to remove one whole layer of the food chain: anchoveta. They succeeded. No anchovies, no prey fish; no preyfish and the big predators checked out, along with the big-ticket celebrity anglers. Today the Cabo Blanco Fishing Club's swimming pool – where once you might have exchanged pleasantries with the world's most famous sex symbol – is crumbling and peeling away, just like the resort that surrounds it.

Although they come at it from different standpoints, big game or indeed any sports anglers' interests are aligned with those of the conservation movement, when it comes to the preservation of fish stocks. Marlin, along with other big game fish, have been under severe threat in recent decades – and not just from the lack of anchoveta. Partly because they are eaten as food; mostly because, as a migratory fish, they suffer from bycatch, accidentally but inevitably caught along with tuna, an intensively fished commercial catch. And so big game fishermen – and fisherwomen – have become more and more involved in conservation. In recent years the 'catch and release' of fish caught by recreational

anglers has increased vastly; so too has tagging by amateurs, working in tandem with scientists. One benefit of tagging is to identify 'hotspots', where marlin and other threatened species come together to spawn, and where they most need to be protected. Another voluntary measure is a minimum size catch, so as to try to reduce the number of fish under the age of sexual maturity that are removed from the overall life cycle.

To make up for the lack of marlin, Charlie decides to go in search of a marine delicacy that is unlikely to be over-fished any time soon, and is also something of a legend in gastronomic circles. It's the percebes, found all over the world, and selling at a whopping £200 a kilo in fish markets across Europe. They're known as goose barnacles; so called because it was thought, before the migration of birds was fully understood, that barnacle geese spontaneously generated from them.

The percebes weld themselves to the rocks to avoid being blasted off by the powerful waves. They have to be chipped off with a metal knife. But that's not the difficult part: the percebes hunters have to do this among exposed rocky outcrops. It's hugely dangerous; plenty of people have died doing just this, the waves sweeping them into the sea. And there is such a serious swell that the local guide decides it's time for Charlie to be harnessed to a safety rope.

Having struck out with the game fish, he is determined to lay hands on as many goose barnacles as possible. His perseverance pays off: Charlie manages to get in a good haul before Jay calls time on the venture, as it's just too dangerous to continue. Tucking in, the team discover the percebes taste mostly of salt, pleasantly laced with an underlay of shrimp. And they've just saved themselves around 100 quid.

The next day, it's time for the final reckoning. The boat that Blowfish, Charlie and Jay have chartered, from Chimbote, takes to sea with a Navy escort. Pirates are plaguing the coasts here, but that's the least of the boys' worries. This whole trip is inherently dangerous because of the effects of El Niño, so the team have flown out one of the best dive safety teams in the world, Special Boat Service veterans Paul Haynes and Gary Humphrey. But their safety briefing, which

ought to inspire confidence, is actually rather terrifying, with talk of recovering 'unconscious casualties' or 'incapacitated persons' before the medic 'does what she needs to do'. What have the boys let themselves in for?

The Humboldt squid is 700 metres below them; but as night falls it will come up towards the surface to hunt. A daytime rehearsal dive is absolutely essential. There is no way any safety team on earth, or Blowfish himself, would countenance doing this at night as the first try-out – it could be the last.

BLOWFISH:

'I'VE SPENT OVER FIFTY HOURS UNDERWATER AND SWUM WITH DEADLY SHARKS, BUT TONIGHT IS GOING TO BE THE MOST DANGEROUS DIVE OF MY CAREER.'

Mindful of Elky Torres's blunt assessment of his chances of surviving a brush with a Humboldt squid – and perhaps of the fishermen's grisly tales – Blowfish is going to wear a chainmail suit over his diving gear, so as to protect him from the lethal Kevlar-shredding bite of the Humboldt squid. As the sun beats down on the stifling combination of 10 kilos of chainmail on top of his wetsuit, Blowfish's body temperature is rising, along with his anxiety levels.

Finally it's time for the practice dive. The weather is getting worse: huge rollercoasters, the raging swell that everyone has been dreading, pick up pace. It's too dangerous to dive near the boat itself as the propellers need to be kept running, so Blowfish and the four-person safety team need to clamber down into a small outboard-motor dinghy, 3 metres below. Wearing, in Blowfish's case, a full suit of chainmail.

BLOWFISH:

'I FEEL LIKE A MEDIEVAL KNIGHT PREPARING FOR BATTLE. THIS SUIT COULD SAVE ME, BUT IT COULD ALSO SINK ME. ONE SLIP AND I'M OVERBOARD AND HEADING STRAIGHT TO THE BOTTOM OF THE OCEAN.'

And this is in daylight. What will it be like tonight?

Within minutes rough water is washing into the overloaded dinghy, weighed down by the chainmail, far too much to bail out. And the storm is getting worse. The team have to abandon the plan before they have to abandon the ship. There can't be a rehearsal, and without a rehearsal there can't be a first night.

Blowfish is absolutely gutted: a lifelong dream has come to naught. No Humboldt squid, and not even the chance to dive. But he is determined that it's a dream postponed, not ended.

BLOWFISH:

'I'M GOING TO GO AWAY FROM HERE WITH A BURNING URGE TO FINISH WHAT I STARTED.
I'M GOING TO GO BACK TO THE DRAWING BOARD AND I'M GOING TO DIVE WITH HUMBOLDT SQUID.
NOT TODAY, NOT TOMORROW, BUT I'M GOING TO DO IT.
PERU MAY HAVE BEATEN US BUT IT CERTAINLY DIDN'T BREAK US.'

CHARLIE'S FISHING TIPS

LOCATION, LOCATION, LOCATION.

Fish where the fish are. It sounds obvious, but you'd be surprised how much time is wasted fishing in completely the wrong place. And all this shades into the next precept.

THINK LIKE A FISH.

It's an all-encompassing, overriding principle, the most important of all, and any experienced angler I've ever met or learned from would agree with it. It comes down to the primeval instincts that kept our early hunter-gatherer ancestors alive. Today *we* may over-complicate things when we're fishing, but fish never over-complicate their pursuit of food. So we need to learn their specific behaviour, understand their habitat, put together the pieces of the jigsaw puzzle. Where would you feed if you were a fish? Where are the ambush points, where you can sit quietly and comfortably and not expend too much energy while waiting for your prey to swim past? It could be the narrowing of a river, a bend, a shelf of shallow water, or near a submerged log, rock or island. The juveniles like cover; the adults may prefer being in a dominant position in the stream.

'WATERCRAFT'.

Look for signs that fish are there. Unless they 'rise', or you can see bubbles, you need to look for the subtler signs. Any hint of smaller prey fish trying to make a getaway. Coloration in the water, sounds of distress, a flat bit of water, birds – they all may indicate the presence of fish. If you watch and listen to the water it's amazing how much you can learn.

KEEP THINGS SIMPLE.

It's tempting to invest in more and more sophisticated equipment, if you have the money to do so. But the fact is that if you can find fish in the first place – see above – and you then use a simple, reliable, strong, fit-for-task set-up, you will catch those fish. If you spend 95% of your time on finding the fish, and 5% on setting up your gear, you'll probably be ahead before you start. We don't want to try to be too clever, in other words.

TRUST LOCAL ADVICE.

However much you think you might know better, you probably don't. That's something we learned again and again during the *Fishing Impossible* series. Sometimes the advice of the local fishing guides seemed crazy. But give them some respect: this is their water, they understand it and they understand the way fish behave in it. What's more, they will help you with everything: tips on how they fish, baits, habitat, specific areas where they know fish are likely to be. It was amazing to me how accurate their information was and how often they were absolutely right. And, rather obviously, where there's a whiff of danger involved, seeking local advice is paramount.

THE TIME OF DAY IS CRUCIAL.

If location is one crucial factor, time of day is the other. Pretty much all the fish that we caught in the series were taken at dusk, or shortly after. That's the prime time for fish to be out and about hunting their prey. An hour in the right place at the right time of day is worth twenty hours anywhere else. At least.

BAIT.

Fly, spinner, dead bait … (live bait was never used in the series). The whole question is incapable of being summed up with a 'one size fits all' rule. Are the fish actively feeding? If so, what do they feed on? What part of the 'water column' do they favour? All these factors can determine what you put on the end of your line. And this is an area where once again local knowledge really comes into its own.

ALWAYS HAVE A GOOD NET.

'Handling' errors are surprisingly common in fishing. And there's nothing more frustrating than having a fish in touching distance and losing it: it's like having your hand on a lottery win, and then it's gone. A sudden shake of the head at the last second, and it can be off. Forget trying to grab hold, this is where the landing net comes into its own. Never has a fish been lost because a net is too big.

PATIENCE.

If you get all of the above right, everything else should follow, so beware of constantly changing your approach. The big thing is perseverance – the longer you keep your line in the water the better chance you have. And as above, best to keep it simple.

BE LUCKY.

There's a lot of luck in fishing, no doubt about that. But as the great golfer Walter Hagen once remarked, 'The more I practise, the luckier I get.' If you've manipulated that luck in your favour, that's a good feeling. And as with anything in life, it's better if you've really worked at it.

BLOWFISH'S THE FUTURE OF PLANET WET

It has always struck me as odd that we refer to our world as Planet Earth, when really it ought to be called Planet Wet. Most people are aware that 71% of the Earth's surface is covered by water. It should therefore go without saying that looking after that vast Biome is key to our future. Sadly, we humans are not known for our good decisions; and we hate having to change what we are doing.

What I am trying to say, in a friendly way, is that the oceans and rivers of Planet Wet are pretty much FUBARed. And even though we know exactly why, we don't seem to be making changes to our way of living. These are harsh words, but there is a way back from the brink, and we each have the power to start turning the tide on this ecological genocide.

There are many reasons why our seas and rivers have suffered in recent history. Industrialization filled them with toxic chemicals, and countries in the developing world in particular still use rivers as a primary source of waste disposal. Hydro-electric power generation through damming is damaging to riverine systems, blocking movement of fish up and down stream as well as permanently altering the flow of the targeted system.

The oceans don't fare much better. Some of the poorest people on the planet live in coastal areas and as their population grows so does the need for housing. Special ecosystems like mangrove forests get levelled, irrevocably altering the local biodiversity and removing storm protection for coastal inhabitants. We are mining the seafloor, disturbing a unique environment that

has been stable for millions of years. Plastics and other man-made materials litter our oceans like hipsters in an organic coffee shop. There is now an area of plastic in the Pacific the same size as the state of Texas. The steady rise of global temperatures is causing delicate and vital ecosystems like the Great Barrier Reef to suffer, to the extent that 50% of the aforementioned reef is dead or dying – 50% of the largest organic structure on the planet has been destroyed due to our lustful relationship with carbon.

The most damaging action to the fresh and salt waters of Planet Wet? Fishing. Or more accurately, OVER-fishing. Since the invention of industrialized fishing in the early 1970s, global fish stocks have plummeted. Shark populations in the Atlantic have fallen by 87%. Pacific bluefin tuna are rapidly heading for the extinction pile due to Japan's love of sushi. Atlantic cod have taken such a hammering that 1kg is a good size to land in the UK ... so you can imagine how Jay felt in Norway landing a 17kg cod! (Which is still small and should be a standard sized catch.)

This is where the bad news ends. Thank Cod for that. The good news is that the rivers and seas of Planet Wet have the most amazing ability to bounce back, just like Charlie's perfectly sculpted hairdo. With a few minor adjustments,

some changes in fishing practice and the occasional intervention from our scientists, things could quickly improve.

We can also change fishing quotas and alter fishing methods. We don't have to stop taking fish from a whole ocean, we just need to identify areas of essential fish habitat and stop taking fish from there and in as little as five years, we see incredible results. A real success story here is the Cornish sardine fishery. At one time, this was a species fished to near extinction. Now it's fished in a sustainable way. A small fleet of boats goes out daily into shallow waters to catch the Cornish sardine, or pilchard, using a method called ring netting. A long weighted net is paid out in a wide circle around the targeted shoal, drawn together and slowly pulled back into the fishing boat. The fishermen can then inspect the fish and return any that are too small, over quota, or the wrong species, back to the ocean alive.

Rivers can rejuvenate rapidly too. Otters, those wonderfully sleek water sausages with teeth, were very nearly on the brink of extinction in the UK. The hideous run offs from working industry had smashed the fish populations, and without anything to eat, the otters declined dramatically. Now, otters are back in every county in England. A complete success story for any fishy fan, not because of the otters, but what they represent. As a top predator, otters need a serious supply of fish. Their presence on our rivers is a sign of just how diverse and replete the underwater menu of fishes must be for them.

So how can you help in all of this? Well, firstly, you can follow the example set by us lads. If you are a fisherman, either with the spear like Jay, or perhaps the fly like Charlie, respect the environment. Don't leave litter, fishing gear, waste, dead fish and other nasty bits of filth lying around. Think about what you are catching. Are you, yourself, willing to catch, kill and eat your target species? If not, don't start.

If you're like me and you like a bit of catch and release, then why not support a charity where the information you gather can be used to educate and inspire young people in the ways of the ocean. For example, The Shark Trust UK want to hear from anyone who has collected a mermaid's purse from the shore. These shark and ray eggcases provide valuable information on where potential elasmobranch birthing sites may be around our coasts

Finally, think about the fish you eat. It is very easy nowadays to buy sustainable fish from progressive fisheries or well-managed aquaculture. The Marine Conservation Society has a brilliant app you can download for your smartphone. With a tap of your fingers, you can instantly find out what fish is good to eat, and what species should be avoided. We want you to eat the right fish, supporting the right fisheries and ensuring that when Jay, Charlie and Blowfish next go out on one of their crazy adventures we come back with plenty of big fish stories to tell!

GLOSSARY

Anadromous – fish that are born in rivers, migrate to the sea when they mature, and return to fresh water to spawn.

Bait – anything used to attract fish, including **chum** and **groundbait**, both thrown into the water, and *hook bait,* which actually catches the fish. Technically, artificial lures are also bait, but the term more generally applies to organic matter. See **Deadbait** and **Livebait**.

Bait ball – when small fish threatened by predators come together in a tightly packed sphere.

Baitfish – small fish eaten by predatory fish (also *prey fish, forage fish*). The term is generally applied to such fish used as bait by anglers.

Barbless hooks – less harmful to fish and easier to remove.

Bill – the sword-like upper jaw of marlin, sailfish and swordfish.

Brackish – water with a salinity between that of sea water and fresh water.

Breach – when a whale leaps out of the water.

Bycatch – the accidental catching of untargeted fish. (The targeted fish often being specified by an official licence and quota). (See **Discard**.)

Chum – bait thrown into the water to attract fish. Typically this consists of **deadbait** cut up into pieces, but can also include other *attractants*. (See **stinkbait**.) **Livebait** is sometimes used, but is increasingly discouraged. Chumming is especially effective in attracting sharks, with their acute sense of smell: but presents a potential danger if they come to associate chum with human activity.

Circle hook – a hook in the shape of a large semicircle, seldom swallowed by fish, and thus easier to release without doing harm. Used mostly in sea fishing – such as shark-fishing in South Africa.

Coarse fish – all freshwater fish except salmon and trout.

Deadbait – dead baitfish, used to catch predatory fish.

Discard – when the result of the commercial **bycatch** of non-target fish is thrown back into the sea. (*Incidental catch* is when it is retained.)

Drag – a brake inside a reel that allows the angler to control the resistance a fish fights against. It should be tight enough to tire the fish, but not so much that the line breaks.

Drop-off – a sudden increase in the depth of the water. A ledge is a severe drop-off.

Dry fly – an artificial fly used to float on the water by means of its feathers (hackle). It is intended to imitate an adult aquatic insect, which lives on the surface, or a terrestrial one that has found its way there.

Fishfinder – an electronic sonar device on board a boat (sometimes known as a *sounder*), used to detect fish, or objects under the water where fish may be congregating (such as reefs, rocks and wrecks).

Gaff – a hook, mounted on a pole, used for hooking a caught fish and lifting it into the boat. Now outlawed in some fishing grounds in the UK.

Game fish – typically salmon and trout or the hard-fighting fish sought after in *Big Game Fishing*.

Gill net – a net hung vertically, mostly used by commercial fishermen. The size of the mesh is determined so that only the intended species are caught, entangled by their gills as they swim through. Also used by biologists conducting fish surveys.

Groundbait – a ground-up mixture (used in the same way as **chum**), thrown, or catapulted into the water to attract fish to where an angler is fishing (the *swim*). Any number of secret ingredients can be used as an *attractant*: breadcrumbs are the most common base.

Handline – a line held in the hand, typically wound around a bracket, without recourse to a reel.

Jigging – moving the rod up and down to imitate the movement of a baitfish or other lure. A *jigging rod* is used in ice-hole fishing.

Keepnet – a net used to keep fish alive, often in angling competitions where they are to be weighed and then returned to the water after the end of a session.

Leader – an abrasive-resistant wire or strong line that goes between the lure and the fishing line proper. Its purpose is to prevent a fish with sharp teeth, such as a pike, biting through your line, and also to protect the line from being snapped as a hooked fish snags it against rocks, trees or other submerged objects.

Livebait – any living creature used as bait, including fish, crustaceans, maggots, worms, insects, etc. Increasingly frowned on in many angling circles these days (especially the use of fish), and of course by animal rights groups.

Longlining – typically the use of lines long enough to reach the seabed, with multiple baited hooks – as many as 10,000 in the case of commercial fishermen out to catch toothfish, for example. Controversial because the lines are inherently liable to **bycatch**, including seabirds.

Lure – an artificial device, fitted with hooks, that imitates a small fish. Or insects, in the case of artificial flies. Lures come in a huge variety of materials and guises.

Mantle – the torso of a cephalopod (cuttlefish, nautilus, octopus, squid), as opposed to its arms or tentacles.

Nymph – an aquatic insect that resembles an adult during its immature stage. Because nymphs live under water until they emerge as adults, using flies to imitate them – *nymphing* – is technically a form of **wet fly-fishing**, but is normally treated as a separate category.

Presentation – a catch-all term that includes the choice of bait, fly or lure; the type of fishing **tackle** used; the casting and reeling (*retrieving*) technique employed; where in the **water column** the bait is aimed for.

Pumping – a technique used when fighting a large game fish, most usually on a boat. The rod is lifted around 15 degrees and the line is reeled in as the rod is lowered. Often only one revolution at a time is achievable if the fish is particularly powerful.

Redd – a depression made in the gravel of a riverbed by a female salmon or trout, in which she deposits her eggs for the male to fertilize them.

Rise – a fish coming to the surface of the water to feed.

Seine net – a rectangular fishing net, with floats at the top and weights at the bottom. The ends are drawn together to entrap the fish.

Spinner – a lure, made of a variety of materials that spins in the water so as to imitate a prey fish.

Stinkbait – organic material, such as entrails, that attracts predators (especially catfish) by its strong smell.

Strike – the quick, strong, upwards movement of a rod so as to set the hook into the fish once it has taken the bait.

Stripping – traversing the artificial fly across the surface of the water in jerky movements, in imitation of the real thing.

Swim bladder – a gas-filled sac found in many bony fishes, expanded to offset the weight of the heavier tissues and regulate buoyancy. Sometimes referred to as the *air bladder*. Such fish are usually dead, or dying, if brought up to the surface, as their swim bladders do not have time to contract.

Tackle – a term, synonymous with *gear,* used to refer to any single piece of fishing equipment: rod, line, reel, hook, net, bait, etc. *Terminal tackle* refers to the hooks, weights, etc. attached to the end of a fishing line.

Trolling – towing lures or baits behind a moving boat.

Water column – a conceptual division of an area of water into its various depths. A term used in angling to indicate how deep a particular species of fish typically tends to be, whether feeding, resting, or spawning.

Watercraft – an all-purpose term for how an angler 'reads' the water and the general fishing conditions, in order to identify a location where fish might be found.

Wet fly-fishing – angling with a type of fly used to imitate insects below the surface of the water. They could include dead or drowning ones, or insects in their immature stage, when they live under the surface. (See **nymph**.)

BLOWFISH is a Yorkshireman, Halifax-bred, the son of a vet who catered, James Herriot style, to the local farming community. This heritage, and an early exposure to the great white shark, thanks to a viewing of *Jaws*, led Blowfish to become a marine biologist. Not just a profession, but an all-consuming passion ever since. He's also a qualified divemaster – swimming with sharks remains an especial fascination. An accomplished bass player, Blowfish is one of the very few, perhaps the only fully-signed up heavy metal marine biologist on the planet.

CHARLIE BUTCHER grew up in Surrey. Before becoming an airline pilot, he worked as a chef in his parents' gastro-pub. He fell in love with angling at the age of five, when his grandfather took him to a local river and he caught his first fish. An airline posting later took him to Inverness, where fly-fishing for salmon became a great passion. But he's equally obsessed with coarse fishing for pike and carp, near his Sussex home. Charlie runs ultramarathons, of around sixty miles' duration, up and down mountains.

JAY LEWIS has lived in Cornwall nearly all his life. He grew up on a farm, but at the age of eleven he discovered spear-fishing and free diving. He fishes at night, mostly for sea bass, off the Cornish coast. Jay joined the Royal Marine Commandos when he was sixteen. Having served for five years, including a tour of Afghanistan, he decided he didn't agree with the values of war, and took a degree in Social Work. He now works in an Early Intervention team based in the county.

ACKNOWLEDGEMENTS

You always hope television series will be magic – but they certainly don't come together by magic. The authors would like to thank all the dedicated and talented people who made the series possible.

Fishing Impossible is the brainchild of Executive Producer Chris Fouracre and Ian Lamarra at Alaska TV with huge help from Jonny Goodman, Tammy Hoyle, Nicholas Head, Alistair Smith, Anuar Arroyo, Ed Venner, Joanna Barwick, Natalie Coles, Marie-Louise Frellesen, Rita Cabral and Julian Watson. Special thanks to Joanna Barwick and Nicholas Head and for their invaluable support during the preparation of the manuscript.

Last but not least, thanks to Hannah Demidowicz, commissioning editor at the BBC and Paul Sommers, the joint managing director of Alaska TV, whose idea the book was. A keen spear-fisher, may he be forever blowing bubbles.